The Complete Photo Guide to
RIBBON CRAFTS

Creative Publishing
international

Copyright © 2009
Creative Publishing international, Inc.
400 First Avenue North Suite 300
Minneapolis, Minnesota 55401
1-800-328-3895
www.creativepub.com

Printed in Singapore
10 9 8 7 6 5 4 3 2

Library of Congress Cataloging-in-Publication Data

Schmidt, Elaine, 1950-
    The Complete photo guide to ribbon crafts / Elaine Schmidt.
        p. cm.
    Includes bibliographical references and index.
    Summary: "Techniques and projects in step-by-step format
for all kinds of ribbon crafts"–Provided by publisher.
    ISBN-13: 978-1-58923-469-7 (soft cover : alk. paper)
    ISBN-10: 1-58923-469-3 (soft cover : alk. paper)
    1. Ribbon work. I. Title.

    TT850.5.S34 2010
    745.54–dc22

    20090241699

President/CEO: Ken Fund
Vice President/Sales & Marketing: Kevin Hamric
Publisher: Winnie Prentiss
Acquisition Editors: Linda Neubauer
Production Managers: Linda Halls, Laura Hokkanen
Creative Director: Michele Lanci-Altomare
Art Directors: Brad Springer, Jon Simpson, James Kegley
Lead Photographer: Joel Schnell
Photographer: Corean Komarec
Photo Coordinator: Joanne Wawra
Cover Design: Kim Winscher
Page Layout: Danielle Smith
Copy Editor: Ellen Goldstein

Visit www.Craftside.Typepad.com for a behind-the-scenes
peek at our crafty world!

The Complete Photo Guide to

RIBBON CRAFTS

Creative Publishing
international

CONTENTS

Introduction

As long as I can remember, I have collected ribbons—salvaged lengths from holiday and birthday gifts, antique snippets from my grandmother's sewing basket, treasures from a flea market, and the oh-so-many impulse purchases of wonderful ribbons I just had to have. I love playing with the ribbon lengths, rolls, and remnants in my stash, organizing the different types, colors, and patterns, and combining them as inspiration for my next craft or sewing project.

I have compiled *The Complete Photo Guide to Ribbon Crafts* as a comprehensive reference to the vast world of ribbon that is available today. You'll learn about the different types of ribbon and the current materials that make ribbons perfect to use for many craft techniques. I will show you how to make a variety of bows, ribbon flowers, and trims. I'll pass along a list of supplies you'll need, as well as tips for cutting, gluing, sewing, and crafting with ribbons. And you'll see how ribbons can be used with various craft components and everyday items to make unique projects for yourself, your home, and your friends. Just a touch of ribbon can turn something plain into something fabulous.

My hope is that this book will inspire you to create your own ribbonwork treasures and heirlooms. You may not have on hand the exact ribbon or crafting supply I use for any particular project, but you can easily make substitutions in ribbon type, color, width, etc. Let the examples shown be a starting point for your own creations. That's what making things is all about—making it you!

A Brief History of Ribbon

Whether used to tie a bow on a birthday present, trim a dress for a special occasion, or decorate a flower arrangement, ribbons have literally woven themselves into our everyday lives. We win blue ribbons (if we are so lucky!), attend ribbon-cutting ceremonies for major events, and display ribbons to support causes close to our hearts. For many centuries, ribbons have been used as tokens of love, badges of honor, and status symbols.

Ribbons are among the oldest materials used for decoration and adornment. In ancient Egypt, tunics were embellished with narrow bands of fabric. The more elaborate the clothing, the higher the status of the wearer. This pattern of dress continued through subsequent eras, including both Greek and Roman civilizations. During the Middle Ages, peddlers traveled throughout Europe selling exotic decorative borders used to embellish clothing. The tales of Geoffrey Chaucer mention "ribbands" used to adorn garments. The ribbon industry sprang from the silk trade as products were sold in the major cities and exported for trade. Rich patrons bought ribbons woven with silver and gold threads and made from silk and other rare materials. Modern ribbons with woven selvages came into being around 1500. During the sixteenth century, the English Parliament tried to make wearing ribbons a right only of the nobility. By the seventeenth and eighteenth century, ribbons reached the height of popularity as a fashion embellishment for both men and women. Men's clothing from that period could be trimmed with as much as 250 yards (228 m) of ribbon. Many of the ribbon manipulation techniques that we use today are taken from earlier examples of historic ribbonwork. Popular Victorian ladies' magazines of the early 1900s featured yards and yards (meters) of ribbon used to trim dresses, coats, hats, and undergarments, as well as decorations for the home.

Today we have access to an amazing array of ribbons and by incorporating them in combination with old and new techniques and modern crafting supplies, we can use ribbons in a contemporary way for our homes and active lifestyles.

Ribbons for a Cause

Ribbons have long been associated with the awareness of various situations and worthy concerns. During Victorian times, black ribbons were worn as a sign of mourning. The use of ribbons has also been associated with various political events around the world, including red ribbons worn to commemorate the October Revolution in the former Soviet Union. In the 1970s, the theme of the popular song "Tie a Yellow Ribbon Round the Ole Oak Tree" inspired Americans to display yellow ribbons in support of the hostages held by Iranian militants. Yellow ribbons saw renewed popularity during the Gulf War and continue today to be a symbol of support of the Armed Forces deployed overseas.

In the 1990s, activists drew awareness to acquired immunodeficiency syndrome (AIDS) funding, research, and support with red ribbons, as red is the color of passion. Pink became universally connected to breast cancer. Today the list of causes associated with various colors of ribbon has grown, and the universal symbol of the overlapped ribbon loop continues to draw awareness and support to many concerns.

How to make an awareness ribbon

① Cut a 6" to 8" (15.2 to 20.3 cm) length of ⅜" (9 mm) ribbon. Form a small loop at the center by bringing the right side of the ribbon over the left. Leave the tails hanging down.

② Apply a small amount of glue between the ribbons at the point where they overlap. Trim the ends of the ribbon on the diagonal.

③ Attach the ribbon to your shirt with a straight pin or double-face tape. Or, glue a small pin-back jewelry finding to the back of the ribbon.

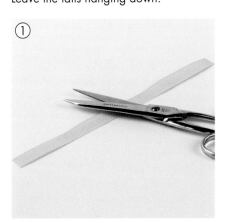

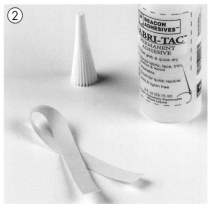

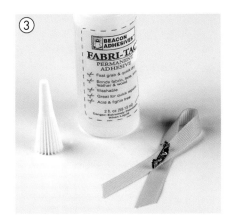

Ribbon colors continue to be selected to represent different causes. Here are just a few.

COLOR	CAUSE
White	Peace, Right to Life, Victims of Terrorism
Pink	Breast Cancer
Red	AIDS/HIV, Heart Disease, Substance Abuse
Orange	Leukemia, Cultural Diversity and Racial Tolerance
Yellow	Military Support, POW/MIA
Lime Green	Lyme Disease, Lymphoma
Green	Environmental Protection, Organ Donation
Teal	Ovarian Cancer
Light Blue	Prostate Cancer
Dark Blue	Child Abuse Prevention, Colon Cancer
Purple	Domestic Violence, Religious Tolerance, Animal Abuse, Gay/Lesbian/Bisexual Ally
Gray	Diabetes, Brain Cancer, Asthma
Black	Mourning, Melanoma
Silver	Parkinson's Disease
Gold	Childhood Cancer

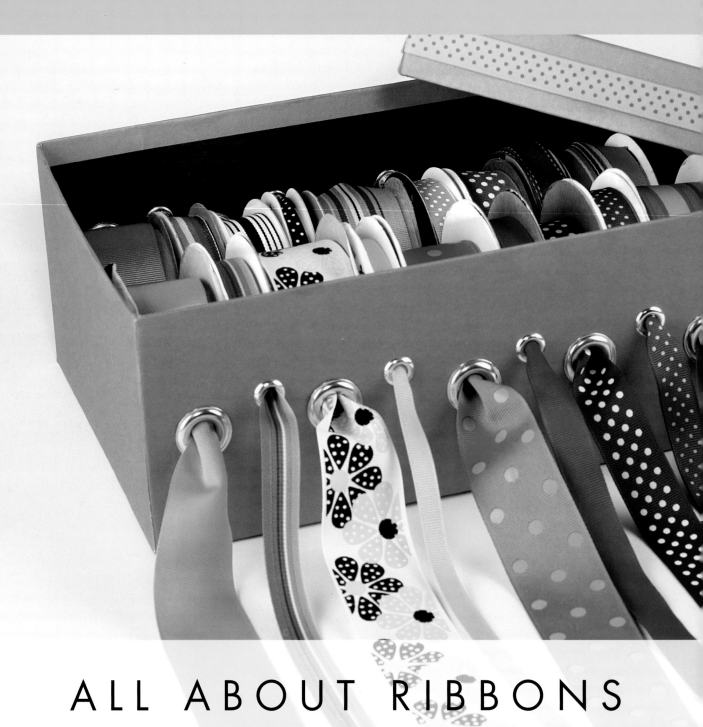

ALL ABOUT RIBBONS

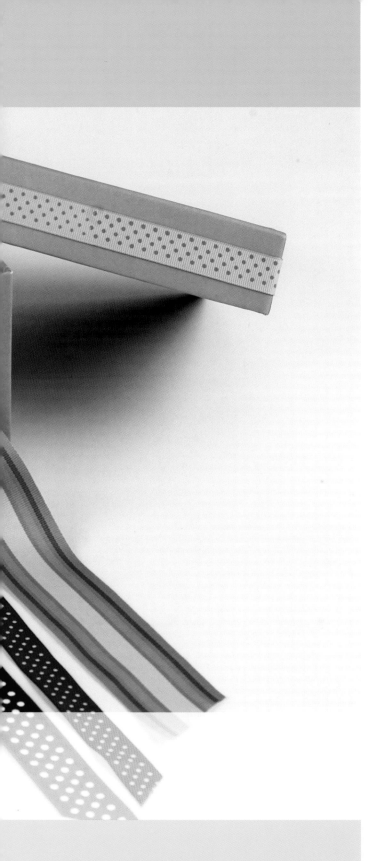

Traditionally, a ribbon was defined as a narrow strip or band of fine fabric, such as satin or velvet, finished at the edges and used for trimming, tying, or finishing. With new materials and production technologies, along with time-honored methods, the selection of ribbons available is greater than ever. The vast assortment of ribbon colors, patterns, textures, and widths now inspires the creation of a wide variety of projects—from wearables, accessories, and home décor projects to paper crafts, gift wrapping, and more.

Different Types of Ribbon

Many names are used to identify various types of ribbons.
Basically, all ribbons fall into one of two categories—woven edge
ribbons and cut-edge or craft ribbons.

Woven edge ribbons are woven on a loom and have finished edges, or selvages.
Many are washable or dry-cleanable. Check the information on the label of the
ribbon, and test-wash a sample before using it in a project that will be washed. For
items that will be laundered, both the fabric and the ribbon should be preshrunk
by washing before constructing the project. Craft ribbons, sometimes referred to as
floral ribbons, can be made from a variety of materials and are often cut from fabric
that has been slit into widths and treated with a stiffening agent to give it body. They
are not recommended for apparel or craft projects that are to be washed.

SATIN RIBBONS

Satin ribbons are woven to
produce a glossy, smooth finish
on one side (single-faced satin)
or both sides (double-faced
satin). Double-faced satin can
be woven with one color on
both sides or a different color
on each side. Satin ribbons are
available in different widths
and are suitable for many
applications and manipulation
techniques. They come in a
rainbow of colors and can
be printed with dots and
other designs.

TAFFETA RIBBONS

Taffeta ribbons have a fine, plain weave that makes them reversible with smooth, slightly lustrous surfaces. They can be made of various fibers, such as silk, rayon, or polyester. Often they have fine copper wires woven into the selvages for extra body and to allow them to be shaped. Taffeta ribbons include ombre and variegated styles that shade from dark to light or from one color to another across the ribbon width. There are also taffetas with woven plaids, checks, and printed dots. Shot-effect taffetas are woven with contrasting colors in opposite directions, creating an iridescent look. Moiré taffetas have a watermark design embossed onto the surface.

PICOT-EDGE RIBBONS

Feather-edge or picot ribbons have fine continuous looped threadwork on each side, forming a decorative edge. You will find this type of edge on many vintage ribbons. A picot edge is usually found on woven satin or taffeta ribbons.

GROSGRAIN RIBBONS

In French, "gros grain" means coarse texture. The weave structure of grosgrain ribbons creates a matte appearance with distinctive crosswise ribs. These ribbons are durable yet supple and have enough body for a crisp appearance. Grosgrains were traditionally used by milliners to decorate and finish hats. They are now available in a wide variety of solid colors, as well as stripes and patterns. Stripes are generally woven and patterns are printed. Saddle-stitch grosgrain has a decorative-contrast running stitch along both sides of the ribbon. Iron-on reflective grosgrain ribbons have a stripe that reflects light and can be attached to any project to improve visibility in the dark.

TWILL RIBBONS

Twills, or herringbone ribbons, are tightly woven with a distinctive V shape construction. Made of cotton or polyester fibers, twills are soft and durable, and are available in solid colors or printed. They are perfect for tying packages or trimming scrapbook pages and can be easily sewn. Solid twills can be stamped or dyed to create a custom-designed ribbon.

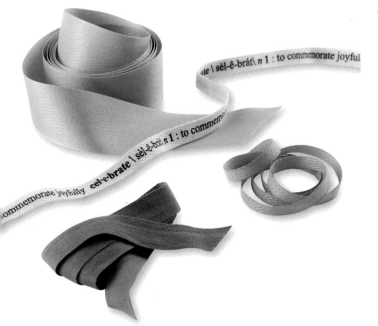

JACQUARD RIBBONS

Jacquard ribbons feature intricate woven-in designs, either in a single color or multicolored, and resemble miniature tapestries. Metallic threads can be incorporated into the designs, which could include florals, geometric shapes, and other figures. Jacquards have a pronounced right and wrong side, and are most suitable for bows and projects where only the right side of the ribbon is visible. Jacquard ribbons may also be called brocade or damask ribbons.

SHEER RIBBONS

Sheer ribbons, which include organdy and georgette, are finely woven translucent ribbons. They are light, airy, and drape well, making them a good choice for gossamer effects. Sheers can be solid colored or printed, and some have satin or metallic stripes woven into the sheer. Organdy ribbons often feature a shot effect produced by weaving the ribbon from two contrasting colors so it changes appearance in reaction to the way the light falls on it. Many sheers have a monofilament woven into the selvages for support. The monofilament is an integral part of the ribbon's construction and cannot be removed. The monofilament edge allows for a bow made from sheer ribbon to maintain its full shape.

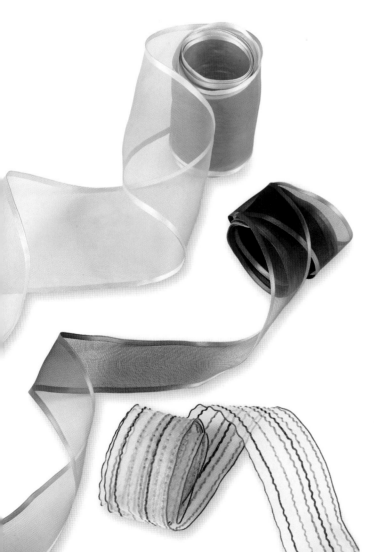

VELVET AND CHENILLE RIBBONS

Like the fabrics, velvet and chenille ribbons have a cut pile that is soft and luxurious to the touch and gives extra depth to their colors. Classic woven velvet ribbon has the plush pile on one side and satin on the back. Velvet ribbons, particularly silk velvets, should be treated with care as the pile can be easily crushed from repeated tying and knotting. Chenille ribbons have a pattern of cut pile tufts, reminiscent of chenille bedspreads.

SILK RIBBONS

Silk ribbons are soft and luxurious. Look for vintage inspired double-sided silk satins for special bridal or heirloom projects. Narrow woven silk ribbons are available specifically for ribbon embroidery. Although they look delicate, they are sturdy enough to be pulled repeatedly through fabric without suffering damage. Bias-cut silk ribbons are cut in diagonal strips from bolts of silk fabric and sewn together to provide long, narrow strips. They do not have a woven edge. Bias-cut silks are often hand-dyed with variegated colors. Shibori-pleated and hand-dyed silk ribbons make amazingly beautiful ribbon flowers. Silk ribbons pleat, gather or ruche, and drape well.

METALLIC RIBBONS

These glitzy ribbons are made with metallic threads, either used alone or with other fibers. Metallic ribbons can be woven or cut-edge. The metallic threads can create a decorative edge or all-over design. Metallic ribbons can also be printed with patterns. Originally, woven metallic ribbons were made from actual gold or silver threads, and were worn only by royalty or church hierarchy. Today's metallic ribbons are available in a wide variety of patterns, textures, and widths.

WIRE-EDGE RIBBONS

Wire-edge ribbons are constructed with fine flexible wires placed along both sides, in the selvages' edges. This helps the ribbon hold its shape when made into a bow. Wire-edge ribbons are often used to make ribbon flowers. By pulling on the wires, the ribbons can be gathered for a ruffled effect. If you do not want the wires, they can be pulled out altogether. Merrowed-edge ribbons are made with wires fused to the ribbon edges or covered with close satin stitching.

CRAFT AND GIFT WRAP RIBBONS

These ribbons are made from synthetic materials and are shiny on one side and matte on the other. They have cut, rather than woven, edges and can be slit for decorative effects with a ribbon shredder. Some polypropylene ribbons are weather resistant. Premade bows make for quick and easy gift wrapping. Narrow curling ribbon comes in many solid colors, as well as prints, metallic, and holographic styles. Curling ribbons are coated or crimped so that they will coil into tight ringlets when drawn across a hard edge, such as the dull side of a scissor blade.

PAPER, JUTE, AND ECO-FRIENDLY RIBBONS

Ribbons made from natural materials, such as paper and jute, sometimes in combination with other fibers, have been developed to be eco-friendly and look wonderful on gift wrapping and other craft projects. Recycled plastic bottles are now used for making grosgrain ribbon. Beautiful shades of satin ribbon are available that have been processed with environmentally friendly dye.

KNITTING RIBBONS

When looking for ribbons, do not overlook the knitting department or yarn store. There you will find novelty synthetic and natural fiber knitting ribbons or tape yarns in wonderful colors. Of course they are great for knitting and crochet, but they also make interesting additions to many sewing and craft projects. Because they are sold in a ball or skein, they are good for projects that need lots of yardage. Knitting ribbons can be tubular or woven flat, and some have a bias tape appearance. Ladder yarns, also known as train-track yarns, are constructed like little ladders with horizontal strips of material suspended between two thinner threads and space between each row.

PREMADE RIBBON EMBELLISHMENTS

Small premade bows and ribbon roses, along with novelty embellishments fashioned from ribbon, are a quick and easy way to add a touch of ribbon to sewing and craft projects.

Ribbon Widths

Ribbons are available in a wide variety of widths—from 1/16" to 6" (1.5 to 152 mm), and even wider. The width of the ribbon is often printed on the spool in inches and/or millimeters. If the ribbon is being sold by the spool, the length of the ribbon will be printed on the label. The fiber content and washing instructions might also be on the label.

Sometimes ribbons are given a number to describe the width. This number is based on the French "ligne" unit of measurement. The ligne is about 1/11" (0.6 mm) wide.

Width 1 = 1/4", 3/16", 1/8"

Width 1H = 3/8", 5/16"

Width 2 = 1/2", 7/16"

Width 3 = 5/8", 9/16"

Width 5 = 1", 7/8"

Width 9 = 1 1/2", 1 7/16", 1 3/8", 1 5/16", 1 1/4"

Width 16 = 2 1/4", 2"

Width 40 = 3", 2 5/8", 2 1/2"

RIBBON CONVERSION CHART

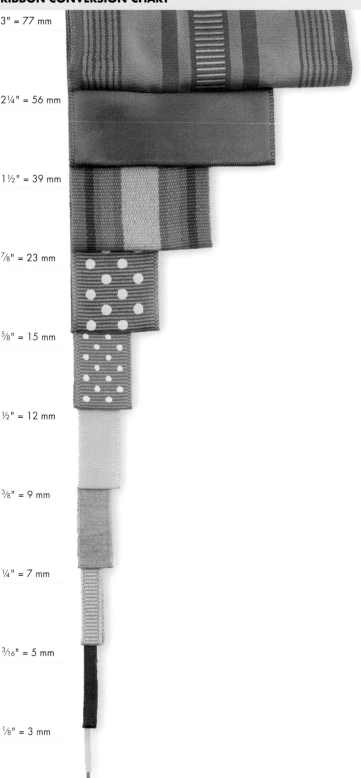

3" = 77 mm

2 1/4" = 56 mm

1 1/2" = 39 mm

7/8" = 23 mm

5/8" = 15 mm

1/2" = 12 mm

3/8" = 9 mm

1/4" = 7 mm

3/16" = 5 mm

1/8" = 3 mm

1/16" = 1.5 mm

Tools and Supplies for Working with Ribbons

Everything you need to work with ribbons is easily available at craft and sewing stores. You may find that you already have many of these tools and supplies at hand.

SCISSORS

Scissors must be sharp to cleanly cut ribbon. Use good-quality sewing shears to neatly cut woven ribbons. Make sure that these scissors are reserved for cutting fabric and ribbons only. Protect them and have them sharpened regularly. The one exception to this rule is when you want to cut wire-edge and metallic ribbons or craft and paper ribbons. Non-woven materials, thin wires, and metal threads in ribbons can rapidly dull and ruin good shears. Devote a pair of sharp everyday crafting scissors for cutting these ribbons. They are inexpensive, and when they are no longer sharp enough to make a clean cut, they can still be used for cutting paper.

Special ribbon-cutting scissors, designed for the millinery industry, have very sharp and finely serrated edges. Keep them in their protective sheath so they stay sharp.

ADHESIVES

Glue

Fabric glue bonds ribbons to fabric and other surfaces and quickly dries clear. It is permanent and washable 24 hours after application. Fabric glue sticks are helpful for temporarily positioning ribbons onto a project before stitching. Specialty glues are available for gluing ribbon to metal charms, flip-flops, and many crafting materials. Hot glue guns and glue sticks can be used to hold ribbons and bows in place in floral and other home décor projects. Always test glue on the selected ribbon and surface to make sure the bond is strong, and any visible ribbon is not stained.

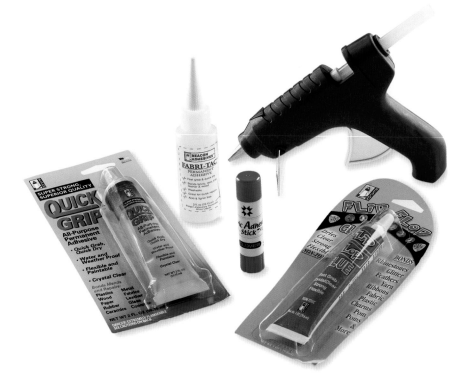

Adhesive tapes

Double-sided Sealah tape is pressure-sensitive and holds like glue but without the mess. It is available in several widths that match various ribbon widths, and can be used on fabric and other surfaces. It is can be repositioned when first applied but is permanent when allowed to cure for 24 hours. It is washable and will not yellow over time or change the color of the ribbon. It is a great alternative for no-sew ribbon projects.

Adhesive tapes, such as Heat n Bond and Fabric Fuse, are activated by the heat of an iron. Follow manufacturer's instructions for ironing temperature and timing. Do not sew through adhesive tapes as the glue will gum up the needle.

Peel-and-stick adhesive tape and adhesive-glue-dot dispensers attach ribbons neatly to paper and other crafting materials.

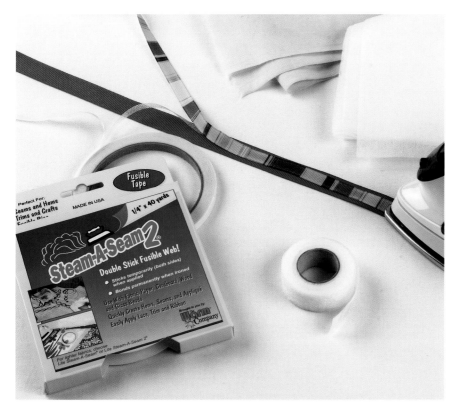

Fusible webbing and interfacing

When ironed, fusible webbing bonds ribbon to fabric, paper, and other surfaces. It is available in the sewing store in various width rolls as well as by the yard (meter). Follow manufacturer's instructions to fuse ribbon with fusible webbing. Sticky double-sided fusible webbing will temporarily hold a ribbon in place until heat is applied. Fused ribbons can be sewn by hand or machine without the adhesive gumming up the needle. Fusible interfacings have heat-activated adhesive dots on one side and are useful for ribbon weaving and patchwork techniques. Use a pressing cloth to protect the bottom of the iron from the adhesive.

Irons and ironing tools

A household iron is needed to press wrinkled ribbons, set pleats, and apply heat-activated adhesives and fusible webbing. Always check the fiber content of any ribbon you are ironing to make sure the iron is set to the correct temperature. A padded ironing board provides a pinnable working surface for holding ribbons in place. A pressing cloth protects delicate and printed ribbons from the heat of the iron, and keeps the bottom of the iron free from excess adhesives. A mini iron is also handy for pressing ribbon. With a cutting tool attachment, the mini iron can heat-seal ribbon ends.

MEASURING TOOLS

Rulers, tape measures, and sewing gauges measure ribbon lengths and aid in cutting straight edges. A wide clear ruler will assure that ribbon rows are kept parallel when applied to a project. Always remember the important rule— measure twice, cut once.

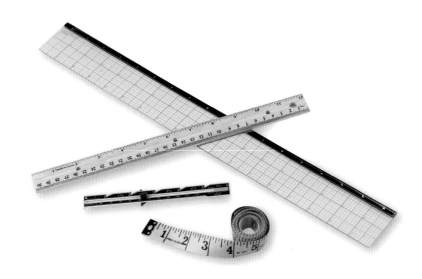

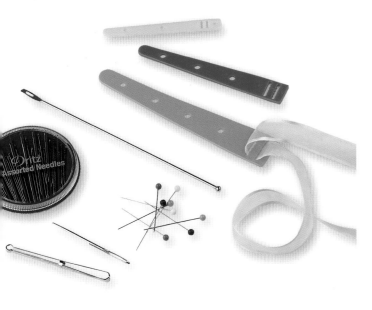

NEEDLES, PINS, BODKINS, AND THREADERS

Use thin, sharp pins and needles when sewing with ribbons. A dull pin or needle can easily snag a ribbon. Use blunt-end tapestry needles, bodkins, or elastic guides for weaving ribbons and sliding them through casings.

SEWING MACHINE AND THREAD

A sewing machine is not necessary for most of the projects in this book, but it is handy for making ribbon trims or attaching ribbons to projects that will receive a lot of wear. Test the selected thread you want to use to make sure it matches the ribbon well. Always make sure to use a sharp needle that will not snag the ribbon. The needle should be small enough to stitch through the ribbon and background fabric but it should not leave too large a hole.

Finishing Ribbon Ends

The cut ends of ribbon should be neatly finished for decorative and functional reasons. Since many ribbons fray or unravel at the cut end, there are several ways to cut and seal ribbon ends.

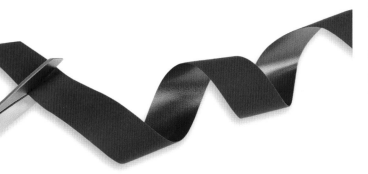

RIBBON CUTS

Straight cut

If a ribbon is made from a nonwoven material or will not fray, it can be cut straight across.

Diagonal cut

A diagonal cut will limit fraying and is good to use on a ribbon end that will not receive a great deal of wear and tear. This angled cut is made on a 45-degree angle, going from one selvage to the other.

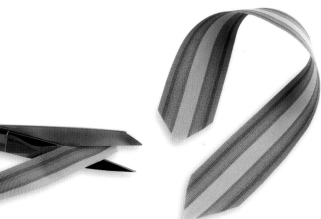

Ribbon point

The cut end of the ribbon can be trimmed into a point. For a balanced point, fold the ribbon in half and cut from the selvages, angling down to the fold.

V cut

The V cut, also known as the dovetail or fishtail, is the opposite of the ribbon point. Fold the ribbon in half and cut from the fold, angling down to the selvages.

A double dovetail can be made by folding the ribbon in half and then folding both selvages back up to the fold. Cut from the center fold, angling out to the sides. Depending upon the angle, the end will be cut into an M or a W.

Pinked ends and decorative cuts

Traditional pinking shears used for sewing, and decorative rotary cutters designed with blades for cutting fabric, can be used to cut and finish ribbon ends.

Frayed ends

Some woven ribbons look very pretty when they are encouraged to unravel, especially if they are woven with two colors of thread. Make a straight cut and pull the crosswise threads. A pin may help to remove the threads. To prevent further raveling, a line of small zigzag stitches can be sewn at the top of the frayed fringe.

SEALING RIBBON ENDS

Cut ends of ribbons can be sealed in several ways to prevent fraying and keep them neat. If a ribbon is going to be washed or exposed to wear and tear, it should be sealed by one of these methods.

Fray check, glue, or nail polish

Fray Check is a sealant designed to be used for fabrics. It is washable, dry cleanable, and dries quickly. Follow the manufacturer's instructions to apply a very fine line to the cut ribbon ends. Alternatively, a fine line of craft glue or clear nail polish can seal an end. Take care to apply just a small amount and be very neat. Always test the sealant on the selected ribbon.

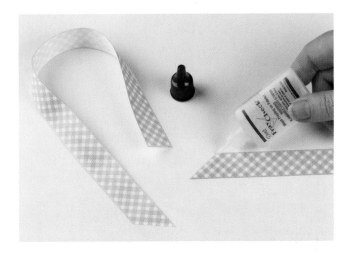

Heat sealing with a flame

To heat-seal a ribbon, quickly run the flame of a candle or lighter along the cut end. Take safety precautions when working with an open flame. Synthetic ribbons will be quickly sealed with this method. Practice and test each ribbon, and make sure the end does not singe and darken. Do not attempt this method with natural fibers, as they will not melt and may burn.

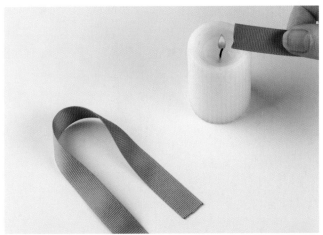

Heat sealing with a heat tool

A textile heat tool and cutter or wood-burning tool can also be used to heat seal synthetic ribbons. Make sure that your working surface can withstand the heat of these types of tools. Lay the ribbon flat, use a ruler to guide the tool, and make a clean cut as it melts the ribbon. Thicker ribbons may need more pressure and several passes of the tool to cut and heat-seal the ribbon.

MAKING BOWS

Bows are probably the first thing that comes to mind when you think about working with ribbons. There are many ways to tie a bow, and with the variety of interesting ribbons available, bows can be used on anything from a gift package to a fashion accessory to a home décor project.

Bow-Making Basics

How much ribbon will you need?

The amount of ribbon needed to make a bow depends on how large you want it to be and what width of ribbon you use. Each bow described in this chapter includes the amount and type of ribbon used to make the bows in the photographs. If you want your bows to be larger or smaller, increase or decrease the amounts. It is often a good idea to draw the ribbon from the spool as you form the bow, and cut it only after you are satisfied with the finished bow size.

Using wire to secure a bow

Many bows are secured at the neck with craft wire—26 gauge works well. It is a good idea to cut a piece of wire before starting to make the bow because your hands will be busy when you need to use the wire.

① While holding the bow loops in your left hand, wrap the center of the wire over the front of the bow and bend the ends to the back. Press the nail of your right index finger against the underside of the bow between the wires. Grasp the wires with the other fingers of the right hand and pull so you can let go of the bow with your left hand.

② Shift the position of the left hand to hold the bow as shown. Hold the wires close to the neck and turn the bow twice, so that the wires twist tightly between your right index finger and the bow back. (If you are left-handed, reverse the directions; hold the bow in your right hand and the wires in your left.) By holding the wires right against the back of the bow and twisting the bow, the wires will twist into the bow and hold the ribbon securely at the neck.

Tips for creating bows

• If you are just beginning to make ribbon bows, start with the simple bows shown at the beginning of this chapter. In no time, you'll be able to make more involved styles.

• Practice the "wire twist" a couple of times. A tight twist holds the loops securely in place, and is essential for a secure, professional-looking bow. Remember to hold the wires right at the base of the bow and twist the bow instead of the wires.

• Ribbons with wired edges can be easier to work with when making bows. You can position them as you like and they will stay in place.

• Double-face ribbon (the same on both sides) makes it a little easier to create nice-looking bows.

• After you make a bow, take a few seconds to arrange and fluff the loops.

Types of Bows

WINGED BOW

This super-easy bow is created by tying an overhand knot at the center of a length of ribbon. By cutting notches at the ends of the tails, "wings" are created. Because there are no loops, this bow requires just a short length of ribbon. It is economical to make for party place cards, invitations, or any time you need to create lots of bows. Select a ribbon that can be easily tied into a knot.

YOU WILL NEED
- 6" (15 cm) of 1½" (39 mm) ribbon

① Pinch ribbon length at the center.

② Overlap the right end over the left, creating a loop.

③ Bring the right end to the back and through the center of the loop. Make sure the ribbon is not twisted or bunched.

④ Pull the ends evenly until the ribbon has tightened into a smooth knot at the center of the ribbon.

⑤ Arrange the ribbon folds, and trim the ends of the ribbon into an inverted V.

①

②

③

④

⑤

Variation

The winged bow can be tied around something, such as a foam floral wreath base or a wrapped gift box. Cut the ribbon long enough to go around the project plus extra for the desired length of the wings. Center and wrap the ribbon around the project, and tie the ends into an overhand knot—left over right and right over left. Trim the ends as instructed above.

Ribbon-wrapped mirror

Use 14" (35.6 cm) lengths of a variety of pink and green ribbons to make this girly ribbon-wrapped mirror. Almost any type of ribbon can be used for this project—satin, sheer, grosgrain, taffeta, and wire edge—ranging in widths from ⅜" to 1½" (9 to 39 mm). Tie each length around a round 9" × 1¼" × ¾" (22.9 × 3.2 × 1.9 cm) foam wreath form. Knot the ribbons at the outside edge of the form, and cut the ribbon ends into a V to create a festive ruffle detail. Add a small ribbon loop hanger to the back of the form, and glue a 7" (17.8 cm) round mirror to the center back.

TIERED BOW

The tiered bow is another easy bow that has no loops. Layering three different widths of ribbon on top of each other creates the tiered effect. This bow is effective on a variety of decorating or gift-wrapping projects.

YOU WILL NEED

- 6" to 8" (15 to 20 cm) of three ribbons in different widths up to 3" (77 mm)
- 12" (30.5 cm) additional length of the narrowest ribbon

① Cut the widest ribbon the longest, the medium-width ribbon a little shorter than the widest, and the narrowest ribbon a little shorter than the medium ribbon. Notch the ends of each ribbon length into a point. Stack the ribbons on top of each other from widest to narrowest.

② Center the remaining length of narrow ribbon over the middle of the stacked ribbons and tie the ends into a square knot (right over left and left over right) at the back of the widest ribbon.

③ Trim and conceal the ribbon tails. Or, use the tails to tie the tiered bow to your project.

Variation

The tiered bow can be made with the ends of the ribbon cut into an inverted V. The ends of the center tying ribbon can hang down as streamers.

①

②

SHOESTRING BOW

This classic hand-tied bow is made the way some people learn to tie their shoelaces—by making two loops and tying them together. Shoestring bows can be tied quickly and are a good choice when you need to make lots of bows for party favors or cards. When made with wider satin or grosgrain ribbon, this simple bow can be worn in the hair or tied around the handles of a gift bag or basket.

YOU WILL NEED

• 15" (38 cm) of ⅝" (15 mm) ribbon

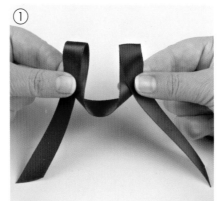

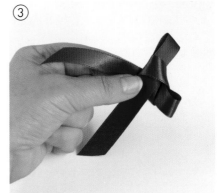

① Form two equal loops in the ribbon, one on each side of the center. Hold one in each hand, with the loops upward and the tails down.

② Cross the right loop over the left loop, creating a circle in the ribbon below the loops.

③ Wrap the right loop behind the left loop, through the lower circle, and back to the front. Allow the tail of the right side to flip over the bow center.

④ Pull the loops in opposite directions to form the bow. Pull on the tails to adjust the bow until the loops are even, the tails are equal in length, and the neck is neat.

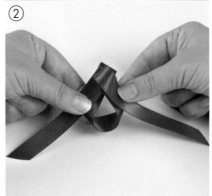

Variations

A shoestring bow can also be tied on top of a starting knot, as you might do when tying apron strings or tying a ribbon around a pony tail.

① To make the starting knot, bring the right side of the ribbon over the left then to the back and up. Pull to tighten. This will look like the first half of a square knot (right over left).

② To form the bow, make a loop with the right-side ribbon. (The ribbon will come from the bottom of the knot.)

③ Take the left-side ribbon (coming from the top of the knot) around to the front of the loop.

④ Then form a loop and place it behind the first loop.

⑤ The loops of the completed bow will lie straight across if you remember to begin tying the bow with the ribbon coming from the bottom of the starting knot.

The single-loop bow is another variation of the shoestring bow.

① Begin with the starting knot as above and make a loop with the ribbon coming from the bottom of the knot.

② Take the ribbon coming from the top of the knot around the front of the loop and slip it behind the loop.

③ Pull the ends and this will form a bow with only one loop. A single-loop bow looks casually elegant when tied on a small nosegay of flowers.

TWO-LOOP BOW

This is a simple bow to make and can be done with almost any type and width of ribbon. Two-loop bows make beautiful wedding accents or Christmas tree decorations. When making bows for tree decorations or gift wrap, leave the wire tails long for attaching the bow. Rather than wrapping the neck with ribbon, you can add a ribbon rose or flower to the center of the bow to hide the wire.

① Cut a 9" (23 cm) length of wire and set it aside. Cut a 4" (10 cm) piece of ribbon for the center wrap and set it aside.

② Lay the remaining ribbon face down on the work surface and fold the ends in, crossing them at the center of the ribbon. Adjust the loops to the desired size.

③ Gather all three layers together at the center and pinch tightly between the thumb and index finger. Pick up the bow and use your other hand to wrap the center securely with the wire. Leave the wire tails long to attach the bow, and spread them apart to the sides. Or, trim the wires short.

④ Wrap the reserved piece of ribbon around the neck of the bow, covering the wire. Overlap the ends at the bow back. Turn under the overlapping end and glue in place.

⑤ Trim the tails diagonally or in an inverted V.

②

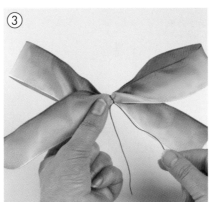

③

④

Variations

① If you are making this bow for a hair accessory or apparel project and do not want to use wire to secure the center, use a needle and thread to sew a few hand-gathering stitches at the neck of the bow.

② Pull the stitches tight and secure the thread.

③ The center of the bow can be covered with beads, ribbon flowers, or another piece of ribbon.

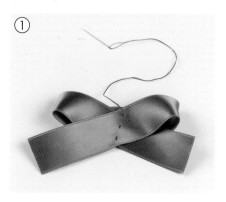

Bows and beads sweater

Two-loop bows accent this basic cardigan sweater. Each bow is made with 12" (30.5 cm) lengths of 1" (2.5 cm) double-face satin ribbon. An 8mm round crystal is stitched to the center of each bow, and the completed bows are sewn around the neckline of the sweater.

TEENY TINY BOWS FOR HAIR CLIPS ✂

Making a mini bow takes only a short length of ribbon. A cardboard template acts as a third hand and helps to make the tiny loops even. Cut a piece of cardboard to the desired finished width of the bow, and cut a narrow slit down the center. Wrap the ribbon around the cardboard and hold in place with alligator clips. Tie the center tightly. Remove the bow and trim the ends.

TWO-LOOP BOW WITH CENTER LOOP

This bow has a center loop, or nose, that adds interest and hides the wire. The two-loop bow with a center is often made with wide ribbon and looks elegant as a fashion accent when made with a sheer or printed ribbon. To make a pretty accent for a special gift, wire a few silk flowers to the back of this bow, and attach the bow to the handle of a gift bag.

THE COMPLETE PHOTO GUIDE TO RIBBON CRAFTS

YOU WILL NEED

- 1 yd (0.9 m) ribbon, 1½" (39 mm) wide

① Cut a 9" (23 cm) length of wire, and set it aside. Pick up the ribbon about 8" (20 cm) from one end, with the right side facing you. Gather the ribbon and pinch it tightly between the thumb and index finger, with the fingers pointing up, leaving the tail hanging to the right, and the working end of the ribbon to the left.

② With the working end of the ribbon, form a loop of the desired size. Gather the ribbon at the base of the loop, slip it under the first layer, and hold the layers together. Now you have a tail on the right and a loop on the left.

③ With the working end of the ribbon, form a loop of the same size on the right. Pinch the ribbon together at the base of the second loop, slip it under your thumb under the other layers, and hold the layers together.

④ If the ribbon is double-faced, wrap the working end around your thumb and through the hole between your thumb and index finger, forming a small center loop. Slip the base of the center loop under your thumb over the other layers, and hold the layers together. If the ribbon is single-faced, twist it once before forming the center loop, so the right side faces out.

⑤ Insert the wire through the center loop from top to bottom. Slip the wire under your thumb, between the ribbon tails. Wrap the center tightly with the wire. Leave the wire ends long for attaching the bow, or cut them short.

⑥ Trim the tails diagonally to the desired length. Adjust the loops and tails.

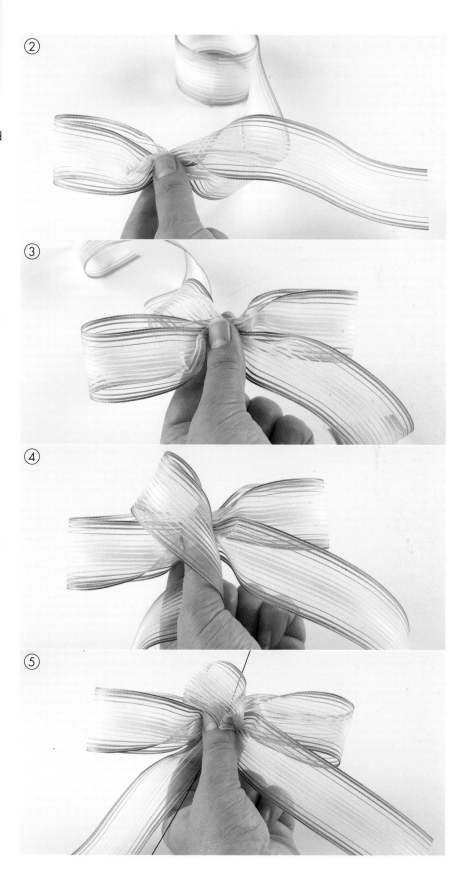

② ③ ④ ⑤

FOUR-LOOP BOW WITH CENTER LOOP

Similar to the two-loop bow with a center, this bow simply has another loop on each side. It has enough presence to be used alone to embellish a gift that is too difficult to wrap. Made from velvet or double-faced satin ribbon, this bow would make a lovely hair adornment for a young girl on a special occasion. In wire-edge ribbon, the four-loop bow with a center would be a festive addition to a holiday wreath. The size of the loops should be in scale to the ribbon width. The bow shown is made from 1½" (39 mm) wire-edge ribbon and the loops are 3½" (9 cm) long.

YOU WILL NEED

- 1 or 2 yd (0.9 to 1.8 m) ribbon, ⅞" to 3" (23 to 77 mm) wide

① Cut a 9" (23 cm) length of wire, and set it aside. Pick up the ribbon about 8" (20.3 cm) from the end, with the right side facing you. Gather the ribbon and pinch it tightly between the thumb and index finger, with the fingers pointing up, leaving the tail hanging to the right and the working end of the ribbon to the left.

② With the working end of the ribbon, form a loop of the desired size. Gather the ribbon at the base of the loop, slip it under the first layer, and hold the layers together. You will have a tail on the right and one loop on the left.

③ With the working end of the ribbon, form a loop of the same size on the right. Pinch the ribbon together at the base of the second loop, slip it under your thumb under the other layers, and hold the layers together.

④ Repeat steps 2 and 3 to make two more loops alongside the first two loops.

⑤ If the ribbon is double-faced, wrap the working end around your thumb and through the hole between your thumb and index finger, forming a small center loop. Slip the base of the center loop under your thumb over the other layers, and hold the layers together. If the ribbon is single-faced, twist it once before forming the center loop, so the right side faces out.

⑥ Insert the wire through the center loop from top to bottom. Slip the wire under your thumb, between the ribbon tails. Tightly twist the wire to secure. Leave the wire ends long for attaching the bow, or cut them short.

⑦ Trim the bow tails diagonally to the desired length. Adjust the loops and tails.

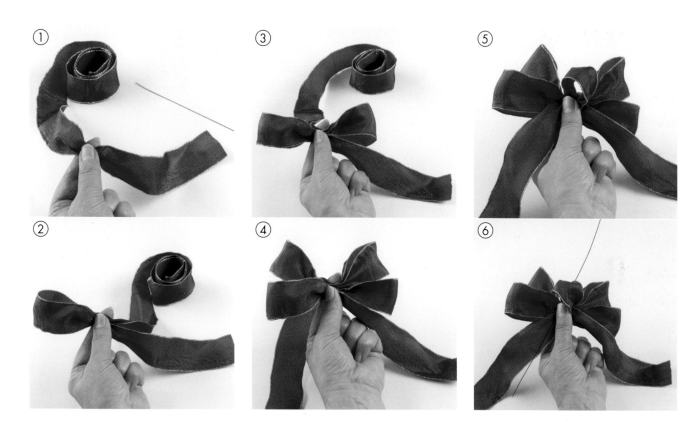

Variation

The four-loop bow can be made without the center loop, and the neck of the bow can be decorated with beads, flowers, or other accents. Turn a four-loop bow into a butterfly by forming four loops without tails from 1½" (39 mm) ribbon. Make the upper loops slightly larger than the lower loops. Wire the loops together with tails made from narrower wire-edge ribbon. String three beads onto decorative wire. Keeping the beads at the front of the bow, wrap the wire around the center, and twist to secure. Use round-nose pliers to curl the ends of the wires into antennae.

LOOPY BOW

A bow with oodles of loops is a cute addition to a picture frame or decorative accessory. A skinny loopy bow could also embellish a small gift or an ornament. This type of bow is often made from ribbon 1/16" to 3/8" (1.5 to 9 mm) wide. Double-faced ribbon is recommended because both sides will be seen. Narrow decorative cords or braided ribbons can be tied into skinny loop bows for a playful finish.

YOU WILL NEED

- ¾ yd (0.7 m) of two colors of narrow ribbons

- 1 yd (0.9 m) of a third coordinating color of narrow ribbon

① Cut a 9" (23 cm) length of the longer ribbon and set it aside to use to tie the center of the bow.

② Pick up all three ribbons and hold them together as a group. Hold the ribbons between the thumb and index finger, with the fingers pointing up, leaving tails of the desired length hanging to the right and the working ends of the ribbons to the left.

③ With the working ends of the ribbons, form a loop of the desired size. At the base of the loop, slip the ribbons under the first layer, and hold the layers together. Now you have the tails on the right and loops on the left.

④ With the working end of the ribbons, form a loop of the same size on the right. At the base of the second loop, slip the ribbons under your thumb over the other layers, and hold the layers together.

⑤ Repeat steps 2 and 3 until you have made the desired number of loops, keeping the loops about the same size with the same number of loops to the right and left. (The loopy bow on the frame was made with three loops on each side.) Cut off the left ribbon tails at the same length as the right ones.

⑥ Wrap the remaining ribbon around the center of the loops, and hold it in place between your finger and thumb. Tie it tightly in the back. Trim the ends to the desired length, leaving two more tails.

Spring floral ribbon wreath

A large loopy bow can be made by using longer lengths of wider ribbons, in a variety of ribbon types and colors. This Spring Floral Ribbon Wreath features a loopy bow that is made with several shades of purple and green sheer and satin ribbons. The ribbons were selected to coordinate with the spring flower stems. This same design looks great with fall flowers, leaves and berries, and coordinating autumn ribbons.

YOU WILL NEED

- 18" (45.7 cm) grapevine wreath

- 2½ yd (2.3 m) each of six satin and sheer ribbons, ⅜" to 1½" (9 to 39 mm), to loop around wreath

- 1¼ yd (1.2 m) each of four satin and sheer ribbons, ⅝" to 1½" (15 to 39 mm), for bow

- 1¾ yd (1.6 m) of satin ribbon, ⅜" (9 mm), for center of bow

- coordinating flower stems

- 26-gauge floral wire

- wire cutters

- scissors

- glue gun and glue sticks

① Cut seven 9" (23 cm) lengths of wire and set them aside to use as the ribbons are attached to the wreath.

② Holding the six 2½-yd (2.3 m) lengths of ribbon as a group, wire them together at the center, and wire this point to the top of the wreath at the noon position.

③ Hold the group of ribbons together coming out to the right of the wreath. Place them at the 2 o'clock position. Wire the ribbons together and wire the group to the wreath.

④ In the same way, bring the ribbons to the 4 o'clock position and wire them to the wreath. Continuing to hold the ribbons together, bring them to the bottom of the wreath and wire them to the 6 o'clock position. Let the ribbon tails hang.

⑤ Complete the left side of the wreath in the same way, wiring the ribbons at the 10 o'clock and 8 o'clock positions. Bring the ribbons to the 6 o'clock position and wire them next to the ribbons coming down the right side of the wreath. Let the ribbon tails hang.

⑥ To make the large loopy bow, hold the four 1¼-yd (1.2 m) lengths of ribbon as a group. Start about 7" (17.8 cm) from the end, make a loopy bow with two loops of all ribbons on each side of center. Wire the center securely to hold all the ribbon loops. Spread the wires out to the side.

⑦ Cut 18" (45.7 cm) of ⅜" (9 mm) ribbon and set aside to use for tying the smaller center bow. With the remainder of the ⅜" (9 mm) ribbon, make a loopy bow with three loops on each side. Wrap the 18" (45.7 cm) length around the center of the loopy bow and tie securely at the back of the bow.

⑧ Tie the small loopy bow onto the center of the large loopy bow. Let all ribbon tails hang. Using the wires from the large loopy bow, position the completed bow to the bottom of the wreath.

⑨ Cut flowers from stems and glue them to each side of the bow. Glue additional flowers around the wreath at the points where the ribbons are attached.

⑩ Trim all ribbon tails on the diagonal.

TAILORED BOW

The tailored bow, also known as the Dior bow, is made of nearly flat, stacked loops that graduate in size. When made from wide satin ribbon, a tailored bow can become a hair accessory, an accent on an evening bag, or a wedding album embellishment. The loops of a tailored bow can be held in place with hand stitches, glue, or a staple. Because it is important to always keep the right side of the ribbon facing out, there are different sets of instructions for double-faced and single-faced ribbon.

YOU WILL NEED

- 45" (114 cm) ribbon, ⅞" to 1½" (23 to 39 mm) wide

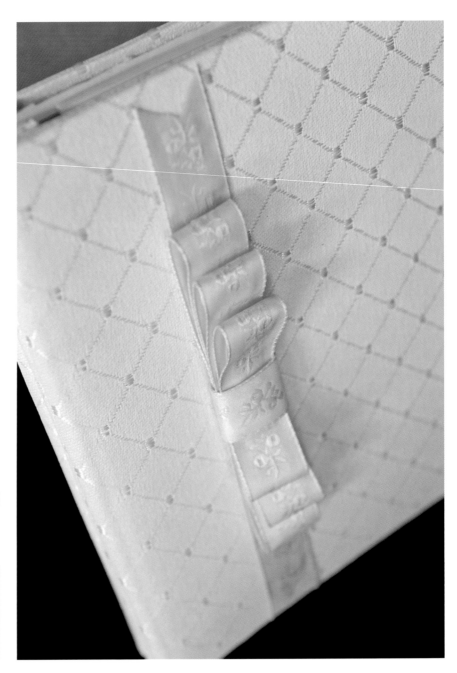

Tailored bow made with single-faced ribbon

① Cut the ribbon into three different lengths, each slightly longer than twice the desired length of the loop layer. The bow shown is made with 7" (17.8 cm), 9" (23 cm), and 11" (28 cm) lengths of ⅞" (23 mm) satin ribbon.

② For each layer, fold the ends under to the center, and stitch, staple or glue in place.

③ Place the loop layers on top of one another in graduated sizes and stitch, glue or staple them together at the center.

④ If tails are desired, cut a length of ribbon 2" to 3" (5 to 7.5 cm) longer than the bottom layer of loops. Cut an inverted V in each end and stitch, glue or staple it beneath the loops layers.

⑤ Cut a length of ribbon three times the ribbon width. Wrap it around the center of the bow, keeping the layers flat. Overlap the ends at the back of the bow. Turn under the overlapping ends and stitch or glue in place.

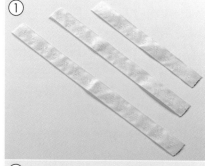

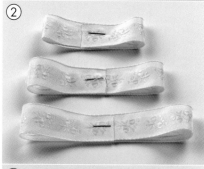

Tailored bow made with double-faced ribbon

① Hold the ribbon end between your thumb and index finger, with the fingers pointing up and the working end of the ribbon to the left. Turn under the working end of the ribbon, forming a loop to the left of your thumb. Hold the layers together flat between your thumb and finger. The working end of the ribbon is now on the right.

② Turn under the working end of the ribbon, forming a loop of the same size to the right of your thumb. Hold the layers together flat between your thumb and finger. The working end of the ribbon is now on the left.

③ Form two more layers of loops, increasing the loop size with each layer and keeping the ribbon flat between your thumb and finger. Stitch, glue or staple all the layers together at the center. Trim away the excess ribbon on the back of the bow.

④ Follow steps 4 and 5 from the tailored bow made with single-faced ribbon to complete the bow.

Variations

A tuxedo bow is a tailored bow with only two loops. It can be made with or without tails. It can also be made with tails hanging down by gluing additional ribbon lengths to the center back of the bow.

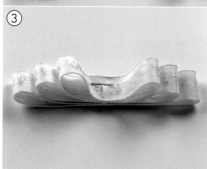

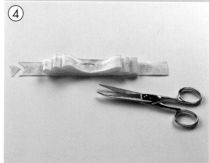

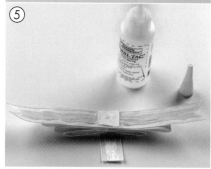

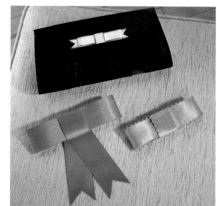

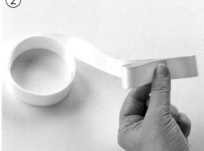

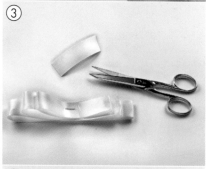

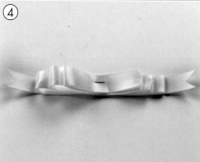

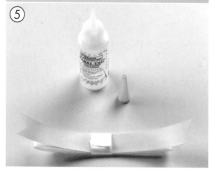

FIGURE EIGHT BOW

As the name implies, this elegant bow is created by forming the ribbon into a series of figure-eight loops, each layer slightly larger than the previous one. The layers are glued where they overlap, and the tails are tied around the center of the bow. Since both sides of the ribbon will show, select ribbon that is double-sided. Look for a ribbon that has a little body so that the loops retain their shape. Double-sided satin and wire-edge ribbons work well for this bow.

YOU WILL NEED

- 1 yd (0.9 m) of ⅜" to ⅝" (9 to 15 mm) double-sided ribbon

① At one end of the ribbon, form a loop by overlapping the cut edge over the working end. This is the first half of the figure eight. Attach with a drop of glue.

② On the opposite side, form the second half of the figure eight and make a loop the same size as the first. Add a drop of glue at the back where the ribbons overlap.

③ Continuing to work back and forth, forming two more sets of figure-eight loops. Each layer should be a little larger than the one before it. End with a total of three stacked figure eights. Glue the loops together at the center points where the ribbons cross. Hold until the glue sets. Trim excess ribbon and allow the bow to dry.

④ Use the remaining ribbon to wrap around the center of the bow. Knot it at the back and rotate the ribbon so the front is smooth and the tails hang down. If necessary, add a drop of glue to hold. Trim the tails on the diagonal.

①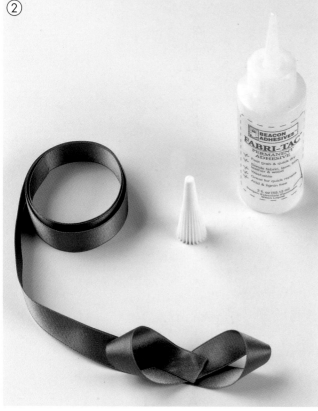

②

③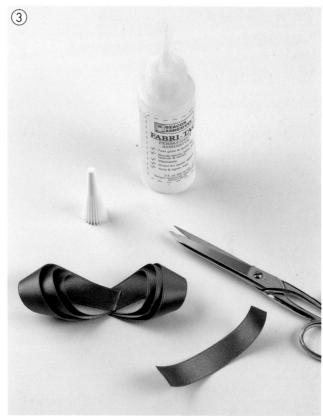

④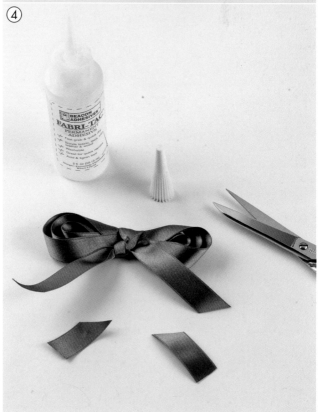

BASIC HAIR BOW

Little girls—and their moms—love to wear hair bows to match every outfit. This basic hair bow is the type used to make the perky hair bows found in children's boutiques. Of course this same type of bow can also be used for other projects, like decorating a gift box or embellishing a tote bag. Grosgrain ribbons are perfect for making this hair bow, and they are available in a wide variety of coordinating colors and patterns.

YOU WILL NEED

- 24" (61 cm) of ⅞" (23 mm) grosgrain ribbon (for a slightly larger bow, use 29" [73.7 cm] of 1½" [39 mm] ribbon)

- 5" (12.7 cm) of ⅜" (9 mm) matching or coordinating grosgrain ribbon for the center of the bow

- embroidery floss to secure the center of the bow.

①

②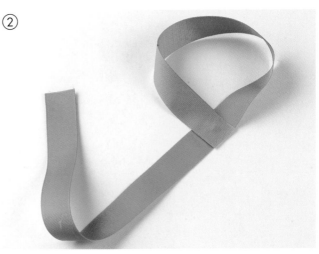

① Mark the center of the long ribbon length with a pencil mark. This will not show once the bow is completed.

② Holding one end of the ribbon, form a loop by placing the end on top of the center mark. This will form the top half of a figure-eight shape.

③ Make the bottom half of the figure eight by looping the other end of the ribbon on top of the center. Allow the ends of the ribbons to overlap slightly.

④ Bring the top half of the upper loop down to the center and hold it at the point where the ribbons cross.

⑤ In the same way, bring the bottom loop up and place it at the center point.

⑥ To make it easier to tie the bow, you may want to place clothespins on each side of the center point. Take a length of embroidery floss, wrap it twice around the center of the bow, pull the floss tight, and knot it securely at the back of the bow. If no additional loops are being added, cut excess floss.

⑦ To complete the center of the bow, tie a knot in the center of the ⅜" (9 mm) ribbon. Use a drop of glue to attach the knot to the center of the bow. Allow to dry.

⑧ Bring one end of the knotted ribbon to the back of the bow. Glue and trim excess ribbon. Bring the other end to the back, overlap the ribbon from the other side. Glue in place and trim excess ribbon.

③
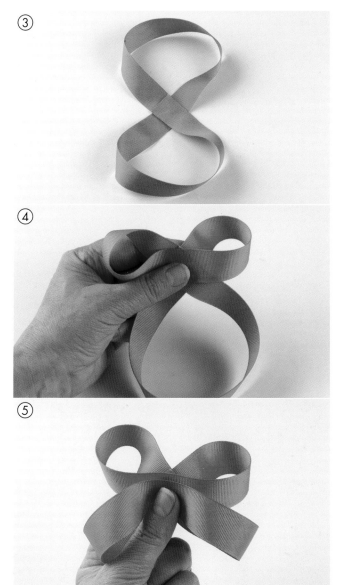

④

⑤

⑥

⑦

⑧

Variation

Additional loops of ⅜" (9 mm) ribbon can be formed and added to the back of the basic hair bow before the center knotted ribbon is attached. To determine the amount of the ribbon needed for these surrounding loops, form a loop of the desired size, and hold it up against one of the loops of the bow to make sure you like the effect. Multiply the size of this loop by 4 and cut the ⅜" (9 mm) ribbon to this measurement.

① Mark the length of each loop on the back of the ribbon. The surround loops

for the bow shown are 7" (17.8 cm), and the ribbon was cut 28" (71.1 cm) long. The ribbon is marked at 7" (17.8 cm), 14" (35.6 cm), and 21" (53.3 cm).

② To make the first loop, bring one end of the ribbon over to the first mark and let the remainder of the ribbon go to the side. Make sure to position the end of the ribbon at a right angle, and add a drop of glue to hold.

③ Take the remaining ribbon and form a second loop, also at a right angle and add a drop of glue.

④ Allow a small amount of space between the loops so the surrounding loops can be tied onto the back of the basic bow. In the same way, loop and glue the third and fourth loops in place.

⑤ Glue the surrounding loops to the back of the basic bow completed in step 6 on page 51, making sure to not glue down ends of the embroidery floss. Knot floss securely around the center of the surrounding loops and trim excess. Add the center knot as instructed in step 7, on page 51.

①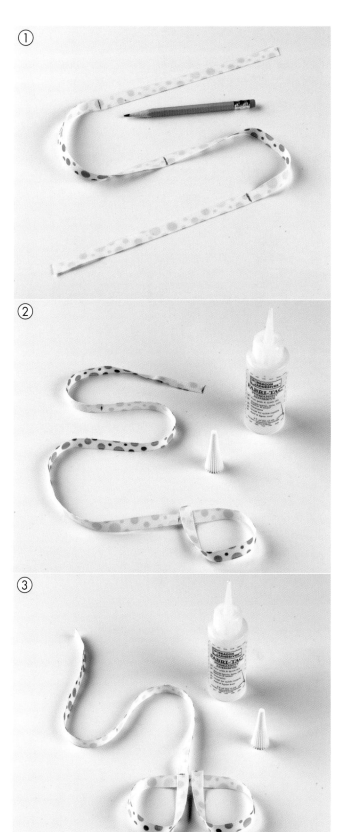

②

③

④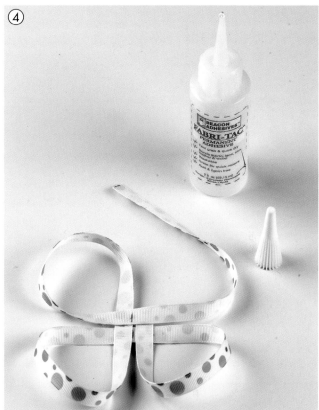

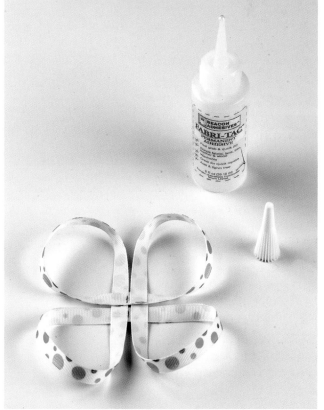

RIBBON FLOWER BOW

Lengths of ribbon are looped to the center to create the petals of this flower bow.

A sew-through or shank button is stitched in place for the center accent. Select a ribbon for the petals that has some body and keeps its shape. Grosgrains, double-faced satins and jacquards are good choices. This versatile little ribbon flower can be used on a variety of different projects, from paper crafts to apparel to home décor.

YOU WILL NEED

- 24" (61 cm) of ⅜" (9 mm) ribbon
- needle and thread
- button

① Cut the ribbon into four 6" (15.2 cm) lengths. Lay two lengths on your work surface, right sides up. Overlap them at the center points to form a cross.

② Center the remaining two ribbons as shown.

③ Insert a double-threaded needle down through the center of the cross. Pull the thread through all the ribbon layers. Flip the ribbons over.

④ Fold the end of one ribbon toward the center, forming a loop. Sew it in place at the center. Repeat for all remaining ribbons to form the flower petals.

⑤ Sew several small stitches at the center of the flower to hold the petals securely.

⑥ Sew the button to the center of the flower. Bring the thread to the back, knot the thread, and trim excess.

①

②

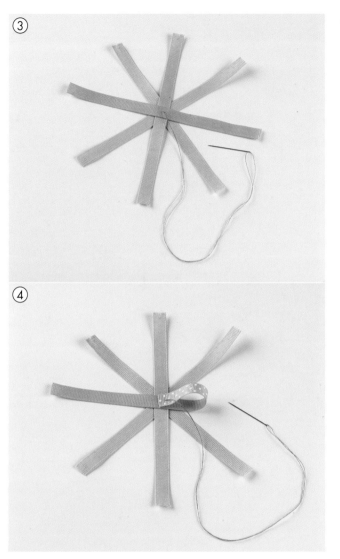

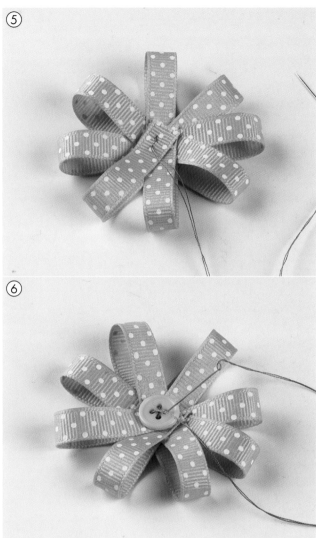

Variation

For a larger flower, use wider ribbon. The ribbon flower can be glued together, instead of sewn. The flower shown uses 9" (22.9 cm) lengths of ribbon for the petals. A 2½" (6.4 cm) loop of ribbon was glued to the center to replace the button.

LOOPS-IN-A-ROW BOW

This is an ideal gift package bow and can be made in any ribbon width, scaled to the size of the package. For best results, use double-faced ribbon. To make the bow with single-faced ribbon, follow the same instructions, but twist the ribbon after forming each loop to keep the right side facing out. Secure the bow to the package parallel to the wrapping ribbons, either across the center of the package or diagonally across one corner.

YOU WILL NEED

• 1½ yd (1.4 m) ribbon in the desired width

① Cut a 9" (23 cm) length of wire, and set it aside. Form a small loop at one end of the ribbon. Slip your thumb into the loop and pinch the base of the loop tightly between the thumb and index finger, with the fingers pointing up, and the working end of the ribbon to the right.

② Turn under the working end of the ribbon, forming a slightly larger loop to the right of the center loop. Pinch it together at the base and hold it beneath the first two layers. The working end of the ribbon is now on the left.

③ Turn under the working end of the ribbon, forming a loop to the left of the center loop, the same size as the second loop. Pinch it together at the base and hold it beneath the other layers. The working end of the ribbon is now on the right.

④ Repeat steps 2 and 3 twice, making each layer of loops slightly larger than the previous one.

⑤ Insert the wire through the center loop from top to bottom. Slip the wire under your thumb. Wrap the bow securely at the center with the wire. Leave the wire ends long.

⑥ If tails are desired, cut a length of ribbon slightly longer than the longest layer of loops. Center it on the back of the bow, parallel to the loops. Wire it in place, forming two tails. Trim the bow tails into an inverted V.

③

④

⑤

⑥

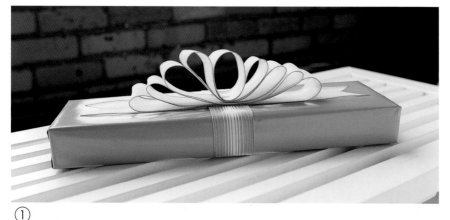

①
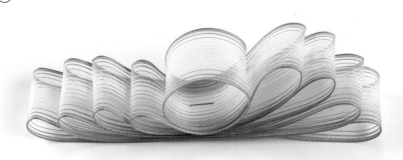

Variation

The Loops-in-a-Row Bow is sometimes referred to as the Ribbon Candy Bow because the loops are reminiscent of old-fashioned hard candy.

① Using double-faced ribbon, follow the instructions above, and make four or more loops on each side of the bow. Do not pinch the ribbon at the center of the bow. Secure all the layers by attaching a staple to the inside of the center loop.

② If desired, add tails by gluing or stapling another length of ribbon to the back of the bow. Trim the bow tails into an inverted V.

FLORAL PICK BOW

This simple bow is wired onto a wooden floral pick and inserted into a potted plant or a fresh, dried, or silk flower arrangement. The tails, which are about the same length as the loops, are turned upward in the same direction as the loops. Several floral pick bows inserted around a wreath add color and texture. If the floral pick bows are used in fresh flower arrangements or plants, the picks should be wrapped with floral tape to prevent the water from wicking up onto the ribbon.

YOU WILL NEED

• 1¼ yd (1.2 m) ribbon, 1½" (39 mm) wide

• wooden floral pick with attached wire

① Pinch the ribbon together tightly between the thumb and index finger 3" (7.6 cm) from the end, with the short tail pointing upward.

② Turn the working end of the ribbon upward, just below your fingers. Pinch the ribbon and hold it together with the first layer.

③ Form a loop. Pinch the ribbon at the base of the loop and hold it together with the other layers.

④ Repeat steps 2 and 3 until you have three or four loops.

⑤ Repeat step 2 and cut the ribbon, leaving a tail the same length as the first tail.

⑥ Wrap the loop bases tightly with the wire of a wooden floral pick. If desired, wrap pick with floral tape.

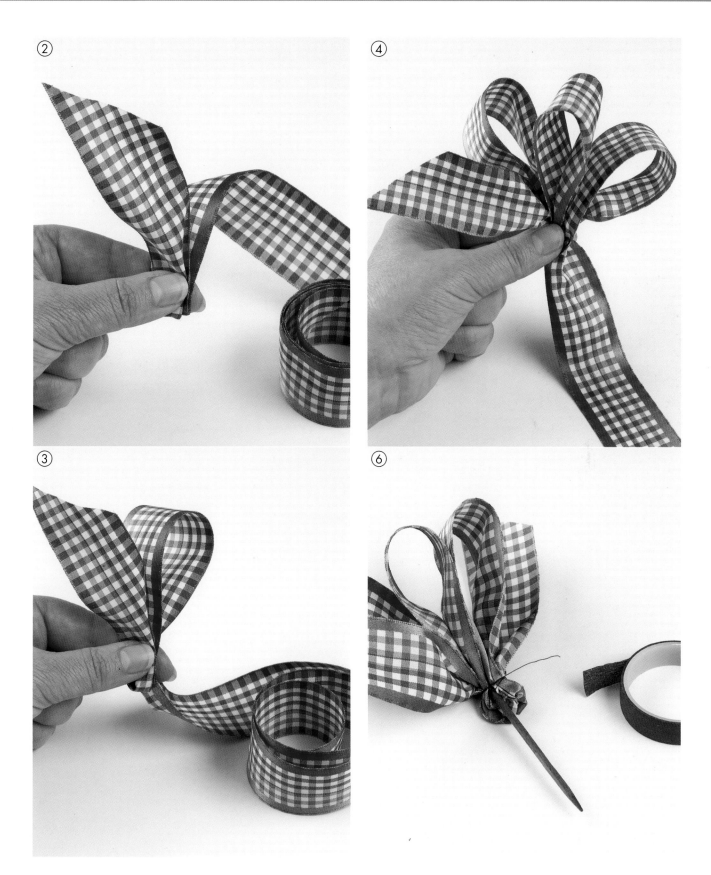

ONE-SIDED BOW

This bow is ideal for a basket or gift bag handle. Three coordinating ribbons form multiple upward loops with a lavish cascade of six flowing tails. If desired, the bow can also be made using only one ribbon. In these instructions, each layer is formed and wired separately and then the layers are joined together. As you become more adept at making the bow, you can form and hold all the layers at once before wiring them together.

①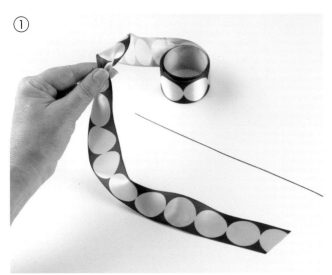

②

YOU WILL NEED

- 2 yd (1.8 m) each of three ribbons or 6 yd (5.5 m) of one ribbon

① Cut a 9" (23 cm) length of wire and set it aside. From one end of the ribbon, measure the desired length of the tail. Pick up the ribbon at this point. Gather the ribbon and pinch it tightly between the thumb and index finger, leaving the tail hanging down and the working end of the ribbon turned upward.

② With the working end of the ribbon, form a loop of the desired size. Gather the ribbon at the base of the loop, slip it between your thumb and index finer, and hold the layers together. Now you have a downward tail and one upward loop.

③ Turn the working end of the ribbon upward, just below your fingers. Pinch the ribbon and hold it together with the first layer.

④ Form another loop. Pinch the ribbon at the base of the loop and hold it together with the other layers.

⑤ Repeat steps 3 and 4 two more times, so you have four loops. Allow the working end of the ribbon to hang down. Wire the loop cluster together tightly just above the loop bases, and cut the wire ends short.

⑥ Repeat steps 1 to 5 for each of the other two ribbons, leaving the wire ends of the last loop cluster long. Use the long wires to wrap the three clusters together. Arrange the loops, intermingling the different ribbons slightly. Trim all ribbon tails on the diagonal.

③

⑤

④

⑥

POMPOM BOW

This popular bow is easy to make. Pompom bows can be made in nearly any size, scaled to the ribbon width and the size of the gift package or project. The bow shown is made from 2½ yards (2.3 m) of 1½" (39 mm) ribbon and is 5½" (14 cm) in diameter. Plaid, pattern, solid-colored, and sheer ribbons can be used to make pompom bows. Several large pompom bows glued or stitched together and hung from the ceiling at varying lengths, make festive party or wedding reception decorations.

To determine the amount of yardage needed, decide how wide you want the finished bow to be. Multiply that measurement by the number of loops desired—a total of sixteen to twenty loops is a good—and add a few inches (centimeters) to overlap the ends.

YOU WILL NEED

- 1½ to 3½ yd (1.4 to 3.2 m) of ribbon, ⅝" to 2¼" (15 to 56 mm) wide

- scrap of cardboard

①

③

②

④

① Cut a 9" (23 cm) length of wire and set it aside. Cut a square of cardboard equal in width to the desired finished width of the bow.

② Align one end of the ribbon to the bottom front of the cardboard. Wrap the ribbon around the cardboard eight to ten times, ending on the back of the cardboard.

③ Carefully pull the ribbon off the cardboard, holding the loops together. Fold the loops in half and crease the fold to mark the center.

④ Unfold the loops. On one side at the crease, cut into the ribbon edges at an angle to within ¼" (6 mm) of the center. Repeat on the opposite side.

⑤ Wrap the loops tightly with wire, sliding the wire into the angled cuts. Leave the wire ends long.

⑥ Hold the loops vertically. Slip your right index finger into the middle of the upper loops and pull out the innermost loop. Give the loop a little twist, and pull it toward the center of the bow.

⑦ Slip your left index finger into the middle of the upper loops and pull out the next loop.

⑧ Give the loop a little twist, and pull it toward the center of the bow.

⑨ Continue pulling the upper loops to opposite sides and twisting them in various directions.

⑩ Turn the bow so the other stack of loops is on the top. Repeat steps 6 to 8. Adjust the loops and fluff the bow.

⑪ If ribbon tails are desired, cut a length of ribbon suitable to the size of your bow, and wire it to the back of the bow. Trim the bow tails diagonally.

⑤

⑥

⑧

⑨

⑩

⑪

Variation

Make a pompom bow with two coordinating ribbons of different widths. Layer the narrow wrapped ribbon over the wide wrapped ribbon, and wire the centers together before pulling the loops out into place. The narrow ribbon loops will form the center of the pompom, surrounded by the wide ribbon loops.

CURLY RIBBON BOW

To make a gift package look festive, top it with a lively mound of curled ribbon. Curling ribbon is available in large spools and is relatively inexpensive. Choose ribbon colors to coordinate with the wrapping paper. Double-sided curling ribbons are fun to use for a two-tone effect. The Curly Ribbon Bow looks best when it forms a casual, tangled cluster.

YOU WILL NEED

- About 8 yards (7.3 m) curling ribbon for the bow, plus enough yardage to wrap around the gift box and leave tails 12" (30.5 cm) long. The total length will depend upon the size of the package.

①

②

③

④

① Center a length of ribbon at the top of the box. Bring the ends over the sides and to the back of the box. Cross the ends and bring them around the opposite sides of the box and back to the front. Slip the ends of the ribbon at the center of the front and tie a knot. You will have formed a plus sign on the top and bottom of the box.

② Cut six 24" (61 cm) lengths of ribbon. Holding them as a group, slip them under the center point at the top of the box, and knot them together.

③ Cut six more 24" (61 cm) lengths of ribbon. In the same way, hold them together, slip them under the center, and knot.

④ To curl the ribbons, open the scissors so you hold the blade between your thumb and forefinger. Place the ribbon under your thumb so it touches the blade. Pull the blade quickly toward you until you reach the end of the ribbon. Curl all ribbon lengths, as well as the tails.

⑤ If desired, additional lengths of ribbon can be added and curled.

Variation

Two or more coordinating colors of curling ribbon can be used to wrap the gift box and create the bow. The ribbon lengths can be cut longer or shorter to create a bow that is in proportion to the gift box or bag.

FLORIST BOW

This is the standard bow florists use in their arrangements. It can be made with as many loops as you like and any style or size of ribbon from 1" to 4" (2.5 to 10 cm) wide. These instructions are written for double-faced ribbon. For single-faced ribbon, give the ribbon a half twist after forming each loop, so the right side of the ribbon always faces out. To estimate the amount of ribbon needed, determine the diameter of the completed bow. Multiply that measurement by the desired number of loops, and add the length needed for the tails and a little extra for a center loop.

YOU WILL NEED
- Use formula above to determine yardage. The finished size of the bow shown is approximately 9" (23 cm) wide and is made with 3 yd (2.7 m) of 2½" (64 mm)-wide ribbon.

① Cut a 9" (23 cm) length of wire and set it aside. From one end of the ribbon, measure the desired length of the tail. Pick up the ribbon at this point and gather the ribbon. Pinch it tightly between the thumb and index finger, leaving the tail hanging down and the working end of the ribbon turned upward.

② With the working end of the ribbon, form a loop of the desired size. Gather the ribbon at the base of the loop, slip it between your thumb and index finger, and hold the layers together. Now you have a downward tail and one upward loop.

③ With the working end of the ribbon, form a loop of the same size opposite the first one. Pinch the ribbon together at the base of the second loop, slip it under

your thumb over the other layers, and hold the layers together.

④ Repeat steps 2 and 3 until you have half of the total desired number of loops. Form a small loop in the center of the bow over your thumb, and bring the ribbon under your thumb with the other layers.

⑤ Repeat steps 2 and 3 to complete the remaining half of the total desired number of loops.

⑥ Insert the wire around the center of the bow and through the center loop, under your thumb. Twist the wire tightly at the back of the bow, leaving the wire ends long for attaching the bow.

⑦ Arrange and fluff the loops to form a nicely shaped bow. Cut the ends of the tails into a diagonal or inverted V.

Variations

For a multicolored bow, work with two or three ribbons held together. Simply lay the narrow ribbons over the wider ribbon widths and handle them as one.

For a two-tone effect, fasten a smaller bow into the center of a larger florist bow that's been made without a center loop.

BOW-MAKING TOOLS

Sometimes you need a little help when you are making a bow—you may be new to bow-making, the ribbon may be a bit slippery or thick, or you want to make a really large bow with lots of loops. In those cases, you may find it handy to use a bow-making tool. There are many different styles available in the stores. You can also easily make a simple jig that will help you when you need that "third hand" to make a bow.

Super-simple bow maker

YOU WILL NEED

- This bow maker is made from foam core board. You will find foam core at craft and office supply stores. You will need a piece about 6" × 10" or 12" (15 × 25.4 or 30.5 cm).

① Draw a line at the center of the lengthwise side and extend it toward the center about 2½" to 3" (6.4 to 7.6 cm). Draw lines from the inside point back out to the edge, creating a thin V shape.

Use a straight edge and mat knife to cut a sharp V shape.

② To make a bow, slip one end of the ribbon into the slot, leaving the desired length for a tail. As you push the ribbon into the slot, twist it so the right side is facing down.

③ Make a loop of the desired size and push the ribbon back into the slot, making sure the right side of the ribbon is facing up.

④ In the same way, make a loop on the opposite side. Make sure that both loops are the same size.

⑤ Continue to make the desired number of loops needed for your bow. Keep pushing the ribbon into the slot and make sure the right side of the ribbon is always facing the outside of the loops. Cut the ribbon, leaving a tail the same length as the beginning tail.

⑥ Cut a 9" (23 cm) length of wire. Carefully slide the ribbon loops out of the slot, holding the center securely.

⑦ Bring the wire around the center of the bow. Twist it tightly to hold. Shape the bow by fluffing the loops and moving them around the center point.

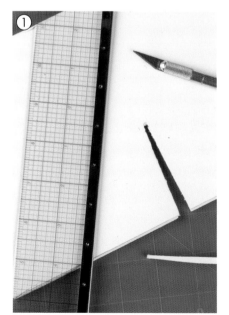

④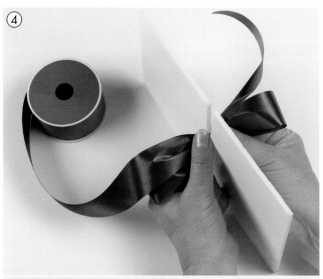

⑥

⑤

⑦

Basic bow-maker jig

This bow maker is made from a scrap of wood and dowels. You will need a piece of wood approximately 3" × 12" × 1" (7.6 × 30.5 × 2.5 cm), four ⅜" (1 cm) dowels, each 6" (15.2 cm) long, a ruler, pencil, and drill with a ⅜" (1 cm) bit.

Draw a line lengthwise down the center of the board. Mark the center point on that line. On each side of the center line, mark a dot ⅜" (1 cm) from the center point. Mark four more points on each side, in 1" (2.5 cm) increments, along the center line. These marks will be the center point of the holes that will be drilled to hold the dowels into the base. By having several holes on each side of center, you will be able to make bows in different sizes. Drill the holes at the points marked, making sure that the holes are the correct size to fit the dowels snugly.

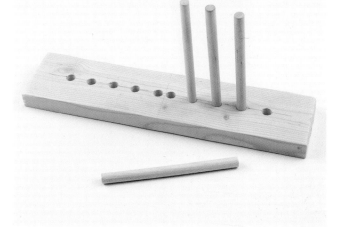

(continued)

Using the jig to tie a shoestring bow:

① You will need two dowels. Place them into the base an equal distance from the center. The distance between the dowels will determine the size of the finished bow. To determine the amount of ribbon needed, multiply that distance times 5. The bow shown is made with the dowels placed in the first holes on each side of the center holes. The finished bow is approximately 3" (7.6 cm) wide and uses 15" (38.1 cm)

of ribbon. Placing the dowels farther apart will make a wider bow and will require more ribbon.

② Center the ribbon behind the dowels and cross the tails right over left at the front.

③ Bring the tail on top of the cross to the center back of the ribbon that is between the dowels and then back to the front.

④ Tie the tails into a knot. Pull the tails to position the knot at the center of the bow.

⑤ Slip the bow off of the dowels, and trim the tails to the desired length.

Using the jig to make a florist bow:

① You will need four dowels. Place two in the center holes. Place the remaining dowels an equal distance on each side of the center. The distance between the outside dowels will determine the finished size of the bow. The six-loop bow shown is approximately 7" (17.8 cm) wide and uses 2 yd (1.8 m) of 1½" (39 mm) ribbon.

①

②

③
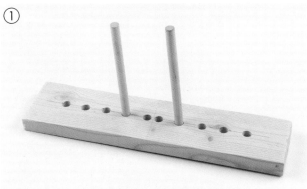

④
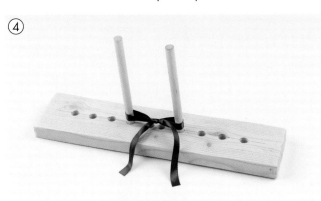

⑤
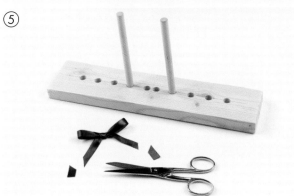

② Leaving the desired length for a tail at the left, place the ribbon into the space between the two center dowels.

③ Bring the working end around the dowel to the right and back into the space between the center dowels.

④ Bring the working end around the dowel to the left and back into the space between the center dowels.

⑤ Repeat for the total number of loops desired for the bow. There should be the same number of loops on each side. Make sure to keep pushing the ribbon down at the space between the center dowels.

⑥ Cut a 9" (23 cm) length of wire. Carefully lift the bow off the dowels,

making sure to hold the center securely. Wrap the center tightly with the wire.

⑦ If a center loop is desired, make a small loop and wrap the wire around it to secure. Trim the tails the desired length.

②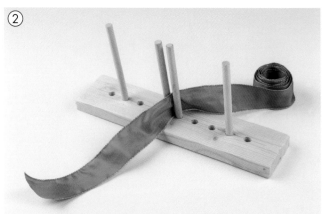

⑤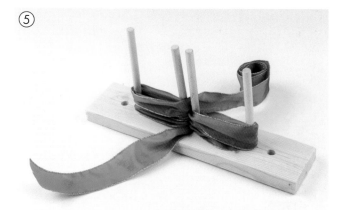

③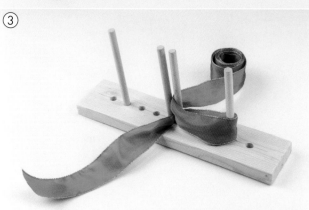

⑥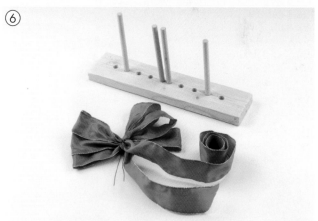

④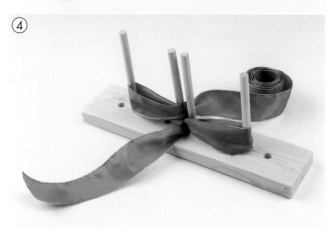

⑦

STARBURST BOW

The starburst bow is an adaptation of the florist bow and adds a special touch to floral arrangements or gift packages. The bow is made in stages, with the loops radiating from the center and short V-cut tails at the top and bottom. Elegant wire-edge silk ribbon is used to accent this autumn swag.

① Cut a 9" (23 cm) length of wire and set it aside. Pick up the end of the ribbon in your hand with the right side facing you. Gather the ribbon and pinch it tightly between the thumb and index finger, with the fingers pointing up, leaving the working end of the ribbon to the right.

② With the working end of the ribbon, form a loop of the desired size. Gather the ribbon at the base of the loop, slip it under the thumb over the first layer, and hold the layers together. Now you have one loop to the right.

③ With the working end of the ribbon, form a loop of the same size on the left. Pinch the ribbon together at the base of the second loop, slip it under your thumb over the other layers, and hold the layers together.

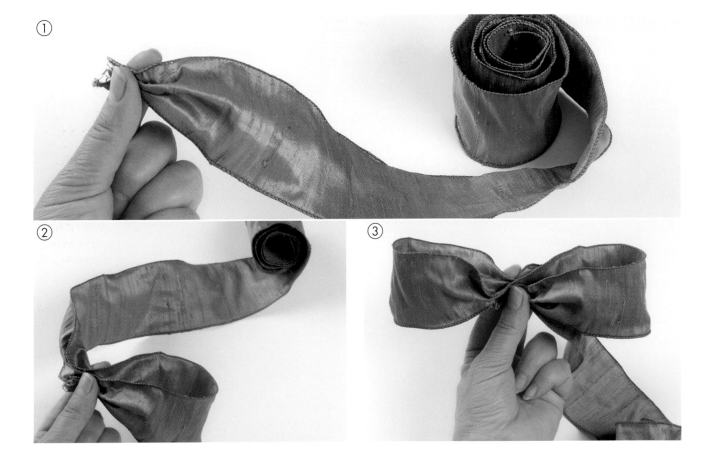

YOU WILL NEED

- 2 yd (1.8 m) ribbon, 2½" (64 mm) wide

④ Repeat steps 1 and 2, to form a second set of loops, and hold them alongside the first set. Cut off the excess ribbon.

⑤ Wrap the neck of the bow tightly with wire.

⑥ Cut two 14" (35.6 cm) lengths of ribbon. Holding the bow with the loops to the right and left, gather the 14" (35.6 cm) ribbons in the center and wire one to the top and one to the bottom of the bow. You now have two tails at the top and two tails at the bottom of the bow.

⑦ Cut a 5" (12.7 cm) length of ribbon. Wrap the 5" (12.7 cm) piece of ribbon around the neck of the bow, covering the wire. Overlap the ends at the bow back. Turn under the overlapping end and glue in place.

⑧ Trim the bow tails into an inverted V, leaving them slightly longer than the loops.

④

⑥

⑤

⑦

Variation

The tails of the starburst bow can be made with a different ribbon that coordinates with the ribbon used for the loops. The starburst bow can also be layered over a four- or six-loop bow, made without a center loop. For this layered bow, the darker pink starburst bow is made with sheer tails and then wired to the center of a lighter pink six-loop bow.

ASYMMETRICAL LAYERED BOW

This bow has more loops on one side than the
other and several tails extending from the side
with the fewer loops. It is a great way to combine
two or three coordinating ribbons and can be
made with ribbons of different sizes or styles.
Because of its interesting, unequal proportions,
the asymmetrical layered bow is a stunning
accent when placed off-center on a wreath. For
an elegant look at a dinner party or reception,
attach asymmetrical layered bows to the corners
of chair backs. Using wire-edge ribbons allows
for the loops and tails to be easily shaped and
adjusted. In these instructions, each layer is
formed and wired separately, and then the layers
are joined together. As you become more adept
at making the bow, you can form and hold all the
layers at once before wiring them together.

YOU WILL NEED

- 2 yd (1.8 m) each of three
  ribbons, 1" to 2" (25 to
  51 mm) wide

① Cut a 9" (23 cm) length of wire
and set it aside. Pinch the ribbon
together tightly between the thumb and
index finger, 12" (30.5 cm) from the
end, leaving the tail hanging down,
and the working end of the ribbon
turned upward.

①

②

③

④

⑤

⑥

⑦

⑧

② With the working end of the ribbon, form an upward loop of the desired size. Pinch the ribbon together at the base of the loop and hold it together with the first layer. Now you have a tail and one upward loop.

③ With the working end of the ribbon, form a downward loop. Pinch the ribbon together at the base of the loop and hold it together with the other layers. Now you have a tail, one upward loop, and one downward loop.

④ Repeat steps 2 and 3 if more loops are desired. Form another upward loop. (You will have one more upward loop than the downward loops.) Pinch the ribbon together at the base of the loop and hold it together with the other layers. Trim off the working end of the ribbon, leaving another 12" (30.5 cm) tail.

⑤ Wrap the neck of the bow tightly with wire to complete the bottom loop cluster of the bow. Cut the wire ends short.

⑥ Repeat steps 1 to 5 with the second ribbon to make the middle loop cluster of the bow, making the tails the same length but the loops slightly smaller than the first cluster.

⑦ Repeat steps 1 to 5 with the third ribbon to make the top loop cluster, making the tails the same length but the loops slightly smaller than those of the middle cluster. Do not cut the wire ends.

⑧ Arrange the clusters on top of each other. Secure them together with the wire ends from the top cluster. Adjust the loops and tails, hiding the wire with the smaller loops of the top layer.

GRAND BOW

This large layered bow with long streamers is the perfect accent for an elegant event, such as a wedding. It can be attached to a chair back, the ends of a floral garland, or used to decorate church pews. Grand bows are made in layers of coordinating ribbon loops. Flowing tails of various ribbon styles and widths are needed to balance the top and add texture and movement. Sprigs of ivy, small silk flowers, or wired pearl picks can be glued into the bow center among the loops or wired to the back of the bow.

YOU WILL NEED

- 4¼ yd (4.1 m) wire-edge ribbon, 3" (7.6 cm) wide
- 3½ yd (3.2 m) wire-edge ribbon, 2" (5 cm) wide
- 1½ yd (1.4 m) each of two narrow ribbons, ⅜" to ⅝" (9 to 15 mm) wide, for tails (optional)

① Make a six-loop bow about 10" (25.4 cm) in diameter, with 1" (2.5 cm) tails, using the wider ribbon. Follow steps 1 to 4 of the instructions for the four-loop bow (page 40) and add another loop on each side for a total of six loops. Wrap the neck of the bow tightly with wire. Cut the wire ends short, and set the bow aside.

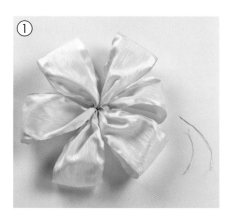

② Using the same ribbon, make a four-loop bow with no center loop or tails and the same size loops as the six-loop bow. Cut the wire ends short and set bow aside.

③ Using the same ribbon, make a loop the same size as the bow loops, and leave two long tails. Wire the loop at the base, cut the wire ends short, and set aside.

④ Make a ten-loop bow with 12" (30.5 cm) tails and no center loop, using the narrow ribbon. Make the loops about 4" (10 cm) long. Wrap the neck of the bow tightly with wire, leaving the wire ends long.

⑤ Layer the ten-loop bow over the four-loop bow and the six-loop bow. Wire all together, using the wire tails of the ten-loop bow.

⑥ If using the narrow ribbons for additional optional streamers, fold the ribbons in half and wire them to the back of the bow. If desired, tie small "love knots" in the streamers at various places.

⑦ Wire the wide ribbon loop and tails from step 3 onto the back of the bow. The loop will fill the empty space at the top of the Grand Bow. Trim all streamers to the desired lengths.

PICTURE BOW

A traditional picture bow makes a handsome accent to any framed artwork. The color and style of the ribbon and the size of the bow should reflect the style and scale of the picture. The bow can be made with two tails that are spread slightly apart, or can be made with one tail that hangs straight behind one picture or several small pictures. The bow is not meant to hold the weight of the picture. Rather, the bow is first hung on the wall and the picture is then mounted to the wall a short distance below the bow, over the tails.

YOU WILL NEED

- 3 yd (2.7 m) of ribbon in the desired width will be enough to accent an 8" × 10" (20.3 x 25.4 cm) frame. Adjust the ribbon amount according to the size of the picture and the number and length desired of the tails.

① Make a four-loop bow (page 40) without a center loop or tails, making the bow in a width that suits the picture size. Wrap the center of the bow tightly with wire and cut the wire ends short.

② Make a two-loop bow of the same width without tails. Wrap the center of the bow tightly with wire and leave the wire ends long. Wire the small bow on top of the large bow. Leave the wire ends long and spread them apart to the left and right.

③ Cut a 4" (10.2 cm) piece of ribbon. Fold the long edges to the center back. (For the bow shown, the ribbon was folded so that the center stripe would be featured.) Wrap the folded ribbon around the neck of the bow, hiding the wire in front and allowing the wire ends to extend to the sides in the back. Overlap the ends at the bow back. Turn under the overlapping end and glue in place.

④ To create a bow with two tails, form a loop at the center of the remaining ribbon that is the same size as the other bow loops. For one tail, form a loop at the top of the remaining ribbon. Pinch the ribbon together at the base of the loop. If making two tails with single-faced ribbon, twist one ribbon tail at the base of the loop so that the front sides of both ribbon tails will show. Wire loop to the center back of the bow.

⑤ Trim the bow tail(s) into an inverted V at the desired length.

RIBBON FAN

Accordion-pleated ribbon fans can be made into ornaments or used to decorate a wreath or gift package. They can also be glued to napkin rings for an elegant table accent. Choose a solid-color or patterned ribbon for the fan. Wire-edge ribbons hold the fan creases nicely. A small bow of narrow coordinating ribbon is glued it to the base of the fan. Additional flowers or leaves can be added behind the bow.

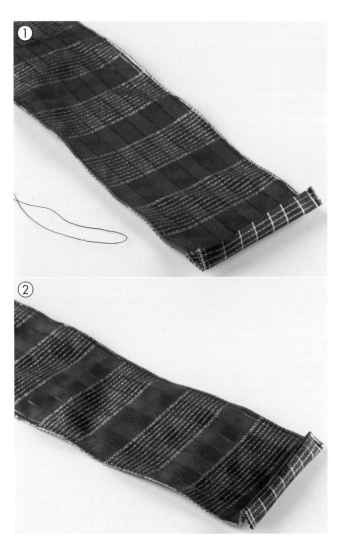

YOU WILL NEED

- 18" (45.7 cm) wire-edge ribbon for fan, 4" (10 cm) wide

- 12" (30.5 cm) coordinating ribbon for tie, ¼" (7 mm) wide

① Cut a 9" (23 cm) length of wire and set it aside. Place the ribbon face down, vertically on your work surface. Fold up the bottom cut edge of the ribbon ½" (1.3 cm).

② Turn the ribbon over and fold up the bottom edge another ½" (1.3 cm).

③ Accordion-pleat the ribbon until you have twelve pleats, ending with the right side facing out, so both cut ends are toward the back of the fan. If necessary, adjust the end folds and cut off excess ribbon.

④ Tightly wrap the folds near one edge with wire, twisting the wire at the back of the fan. Trim excess wire, or leave the wire ends long if they will be needed to attach the fan to a project.

⑤ Spread the free edge into a fan shape. Make a small shoestring bow (page 34) with narrow ribbon and glue it to the fan front, over the wire.

③
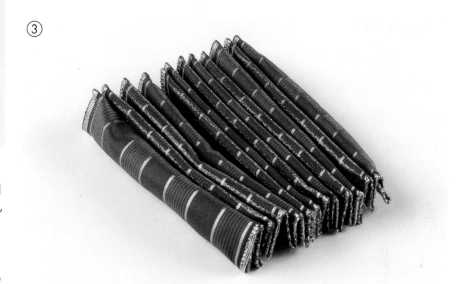

④

⑤
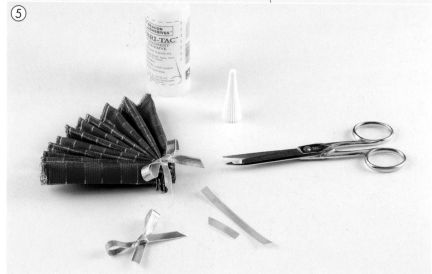

PINWHEEL BOW

This perky bow can be made with one or two coordinating ribbons. Wire-edge ribbon works best because you can adjust the positions of the pinwheel spokes and they will stay in place. The wire at the center of the pinwheel bow can be hidden with a small embellishment such as a button or beads, or it can be covered with narrow coordinating ribbon. Use pinwheel bows to decorate gift bags or boxes, choosing an accent for the center that suits the theme of the event. Make them from narrower ribbon to create an accent for a card or scrapbook page.

YOU WILL NEED

• Determine how wide you want the pinwheel to be and multiply that measurement by 8. The bow shown is 6" (15.2 cm) wide and uses 48" (1.2 m) of 1½" (39 mm) wire-edge ribbon.

①

① Cut a 9" (23 cm) length of wire and set it aside. Cut the ribbon into eight 6" (15.2 cm) lengths. Fold each length in half to mark the center. Unfold.

② Pick up a ribbon, and gather it across the center, holding it tightly between your thumb and index finger.

③ Pick up a second ribbon, gather it across the center, and hold it together tightly alongside the first one.

④ Continue adding ribbons one by one until you are holding all eight ribbons. If using two different ribbons, alternate them.

⑤ Tightly wrap the ribbon centers together with the wire.

⑥ Fan out the ribbons into a pinwheel shape. Trim the ribbon ends into an inverted V.

⑦ Glue or sew a button or small embellishment to the center of the pinwheel, or tie a narrow coordinating ribbon over the wire.

BLOSSOM BOW

The ribbon blossom bow is a colorful collage of different ribbons knotted together at the center. Making a ribbon blossom is a great way to use remnants, and creates a fun accent for hair bows, fashion accessories, or gift bags. To create a successful blossom bow, choose ribbons in two or three coordinating colors. Almost any style of ribbon can be used.

YOU WILL NEED

• The finished size of the blossom bows shown is approximately 3" (7.6 cm). The bow is made from twenty 5" (12.7 cm) lengths of ribbon in a variety of coordinating patterns and styles, ranging in width from ¼" to ½" (7 to 12 mm). You will also need one 7" (17.8 cm) length of ribbon.

① Stack the ribbon lengths on top of each other in an attractive order, varying colors and types of ribbon. Use two clothespins to clip the stack together on each side of center.

② Place the center of the 7" (17.8 cm) ribbon at the back of the stack. Bring the ends to the front and tie them tightly around the ribbon stack with a square knot. It is important that this knot be very tight so the ribbons in the stack do not slip. You may want to use a length of wire tightly twisted around the center to hold the ribbon layers securely. The 7" (17.8 cm) ribbon can then be tied over the wire.

③ Place the stack on your work surface horizontally. Remove the clothespin from the top half of the stack. Fold the top four ribbon lengths back from the top stack. Clip them to the ribbons in the bottom stack.

④ Fold back all the ribbons from the top of the stack, leaving the bottom two lengths. Tie these two ribbons together, pulling them tightly until the knot slides into the center of the bow. Continue to tie two ribbons at a time until all ribbons on the top stack are tied.

(5) Unclip the bottom stack. Take the top four ribbon lengths away from the rest and clip them together with the top lengths from the top stack.

(6) As done for the top stack, working from the back of the stack, tie the ribbon lengths together, two at a time. Make sure each knot slides into the center of the bow.

(7) The remaining lengths from each side that have been held together can now be unclipped and tied in pairs. Make sure each knot slides into the center as these ribbons will fill in the center of the bow.

(8) Use sharp scissors to trim and shape the bow evenly.

Variation

For a larger ribbon blossom, use more layers of ribbon and wider ribbons. Cut the ribbon lengths about 2" (5 cm) wider than the desired finished size of the bow.

POINSETTIA BOW

The poinsettia is the traditional Christmas flower. This poinsettia bow makes a beautiful package decoration. You can also use it to accent a centerpiece or decorate your holiday tree, wreath, or swag. All shades of red or pink and ivory satin or velvet ribbons make elegant, realistic poinsettia bows. You can also make beautiful poinsettia bows from metallic ribbons. Glue small beads to the center to finish off the flower and hide the wire.

YOU WILL NEED

- 1½ yd (1.4 m) ribbon, 1½" (39 mm) wide for the petals
- 9" (23 cm) ribbon, 1½" (39 mm) wide for the leaves

①

②

③

④

① Cut two 9" (23 cm) lengths of wire and set them aside. Cut four 8" (20.3 cm) lengths and three 6" (15.2 cm) lengths of petal ribbon. Trim the ends into points. Fold each piece in half to mark the center. Unfold.

② Pick up a long ribbon petal and gather across the center, holding it tightly between your thumb and index finger.

③ Pick up the other long ribbon petals, one at a time. Gather them across the center, and hold them together tightly alongside the first one.

④ Tightly wrap the ribbon centers with wire. Cut the wire ends short. Fan the petal out evenly and set aside.

⑤ Repeat steps 2 to 4 with the short ribbon petals, but leave the wire ends long. Wire the short petals over the long petals, leaving the wire ends long.

⑥ Trim the ends of the leaf ribbon into points. Gather the ribbon across the center and wire it to the back of the poinsettia bow. If desired, leave the wire ends long for attaching the bow.

⑦ To cover the wire, place a puddle of clear-drying craft glue at the center of the poinsettia and cover with small beads. Allow to dry and shake off excess beads.

⑤

⑥

⑦

Ribbon poinsettia wreath

The colors of a beautiful wide silk plaid ribbon inspired the fun look of this Ribbon Poinsettia Wreath. A traditional holiday plaid and red and green ribbons can also be used for a wreath with a more classic color scheme.

YOU WILL NEED

- 20" (50.8 cm) evergreen wreath

- 2¾ yd (2.5 m) of 4" (102 mm)-wide wire-edge silk plaid ribbon for bow

- 3¼ yd (2.9 m) of 1½" (39 mm)-wide green satin ribbon for poinsettia leaves and bow

- 7 yd (6.4 m) of 1½" (39 mm)-wide fuchsia or red satin ribbon for poinsettia petals

- light green or gold seed beads, size 6 or 8

- scissors

- ruler

- floral wire

- tacky glue

- hot glue gun and glue sticks

① Make a four-loop bow without a center with the plaid ribbon, leaving tails about 18" (45.7 cm) long. Cut a 2-yd (1.8 m) length of the green satin ribbon and make a four-loop bow with center, leaving tails about 16" (40.6 cm) long. Wire the satin bow to the center of the plaid bow.

② Fluff branches of wreath and wire the completed bow to the bottom of the wreath. Cut the ribbon tails into an inverted V.

③ Following instructions on page 86, make five poinsettias with the remaining ribbons. Use tacky glue to attach seed beads to the center of each poinsettia. Allow to dry.

④ Using photo as guide for placement, wire ribbon poinsettias to the wreath. Add a little hot glue under plaid bow and each poinsettia to hold in place.

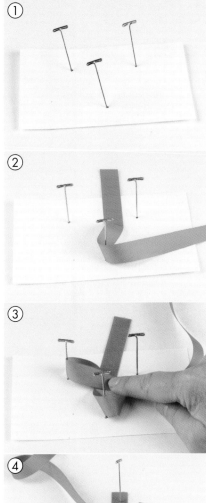

STAR BOW

Star bows look like the premade gift bows sold in the store next
to the wrapping paper. Since gift bows are usually only available
in a limited number of colors, it is nice to be able to make your
own star bows for special gifts and projects. The layers of this bow
are formed by wrapping the ribbon around pins. The pins can be
placed into any surface that will hold them securely—a well-padded
ironing board or a thick form board will work. This bow can be
tricky to do and does require a little patience and practice. I have
found it easiest to start with ⅝" (15 mm) craft or grosgrain ribbon.
Once you get a hang of winding the layers and holding them
together, you can try other widths and types of ribbon.

YOU WILL NEED

- 1 yd (0.9 m) of ⅝" (15 mm)
  grosgrain ribbon
- five T-pins
- pinable surface
- needle and thread to match
  the ribbon color

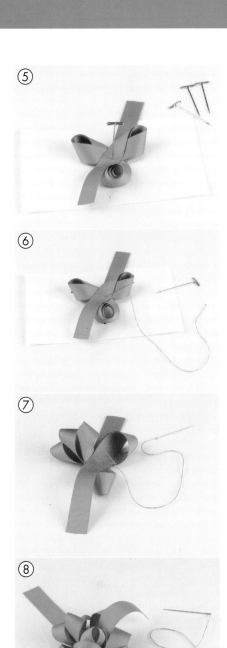

⑤ Place three pins into the surface, creating a triangle shape—one pin on the left, one of the right, and one at the bottom.

② Pin one end of the ribbon about 3" (7.6 cm) above the top of the triangle, and let the working end of the ribbon hang down toward the bottom pin. Wrap the ribbon around the bottom pin, from left to right.

③ Cross the ribbon at the center and hold it with your finger. Bring the ribbon around the left pin, from top to bottom, and over to the center. Use your finger to hold all the ribbon layers at the center.

④ Bring the ribbon around the right pin, from bottom to top, and back to the center. Hold all layers at the center.

⑤ Continue to wrap the ribbon around the pins until you have a total of three loops around each pin. It is important that the center is held securely at each passing of the ribbon. When all layers are wound, place a pin at the center to hold. Make sure that all ribbon layers are caught by the pin. This will be the back side of the bow. Remove all pins, except the center pin.

⑥ With double-threaded needle, insert the needle at the point where the pin is holding the ribbons. Bring the needle from the back of the bow to the front. Do not cut thread. Remove the pin.

⑦ Carefully separate each group of ribbon loops while holding onto the thread coming from the center of the bow.

⑧ Gently twist the loop layers to create a full bow. Take a small stitch through all the ribbon layers to the back of the bow. Bring the needle back to the front of the bow.

⑨ Form a center loop with the beginning end of the ribbon. Take a few small stitches into the inside of the loop to hold it in place. Bring the needle to the back of the bow. Knot and trim thread.

Variation

If using a thin craft ribbon, instead of using a needle and thread, you can secure all the ribbon loops by attaching a staple inside the center loop.

Bow-maker plates

Because making star bows is challenging, I was thrilled to discover these bow-maker plates. They come in three sizes, and they make it quick and easy to create three-, five-, or seven-point star bows. Just follow the manufacturer's instructions to wrap the ribbon around the plate. Combine two or more coordinating bows for a layered look. Decorate the center of the bow with a loop of ribbon, beads, a button, or a pompom.

RIBBON FLOWERS

R ibbon lengths can be gathered and manipulated to make lifelike or fanciful flowers. Basic techniques used on ribbons of different widths and colors can produce a variety of flowers that share characteristics, but have their own distinctive looks. The leaves that accompany them and the materials used to create the center of the flowers help to distinguish one flower from another.

Getting Started

Almost any kind of ribbon can be used to make flowers.

Variegated and ombre ribbons can create realistic flowers. Ethereal, romantic looks can be achieved with sheer ribbons. Wire-edge ribbons are suitable for many flowers. Removing the wire along one edge before it is gathered to make the flower shape may help to minimize the bulk at the flower center. Wired outer edges of the petals allow them to be shaped, and help to make each flower unique and natural-looking.

Flowers that are intended to be sewn or glued to garments or accessories can be tacked to a backing of stiff, woven interfacing as they are being formed. The excess backing is then trimmed away when the flower is finished so it does not show from the front. Flowers and leaves can then be arranged and tacked to another piece of backing or secured directly to the project.

How much ribbon will you need? The amount of ribbon needed for each flower will depend upon the type of flower and the width of the selected ribbon. Proportion is the key. The instructions will state the ribbon measurements in number of ribbon widths needed. This will be referred to as "RW." For example, if you are using a ribbon that is 1½" (39 mm) wide and the instructions call for a length of 5 RWs, you will cut a 7½" (19 cm) length of ribbon (5 × 1½" = 7½" or 5 × 39 mm = 19 cm).

YOU WILL NEED
- ribbons
- air-soluble marking pen
- scissors
- needle and thread
- stiff, woven interfacing or crinoline
- Fray Check
- material for flower centers
- floral wire
- floral tape

Gathered Flowers

The style and color of the ribbon, the pattern of the hand stitches, and the fullness of the ribbon contribute to the characteristics of gathered flowers. Mimic natural flowers or design your own fanciful blossoms.

SINGLE GATHERING LINE

Open-end method

① Cut 5 to 15 RWs of ribbon, depending on the desired finished fullness. Remove wire from the inner edge (the edge that will become the flower center). Apply Fray Check to the cut ends.

② Thread the needle with double thread, and knot the end. Insert the needle into the outer edge near the cut end. Secure thread by running needle between the threads before pulling the knot tight.

③ Stitch to the inner edge, round the corner, and stitch close to the inner edge the length of the ribbon. At the opposite end, round the corner and stitch to the outer edge.

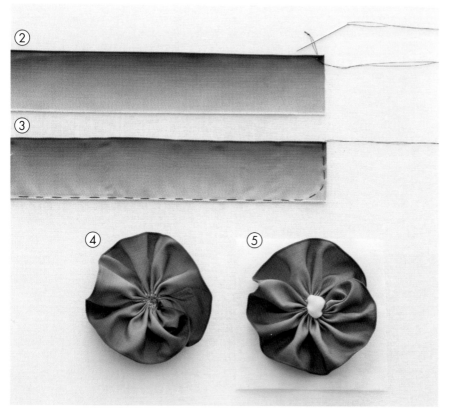

④ Pull up on the thread, gather the ribbon tightly. Knot the end to the beginning, turning raw edges to the back of the flower.

⑤ Tack the flower to a square of backing, directing short stitches from the center outward. Shape petals as desired and tack in place as needed along the outer edges. Add a center to the flower, using one of the methods shown on page 105.

Closed method

① Follow step 1 in open-end method. Beginning at the inner edge, with right sides of ribbon together, form ribbon into a circle and stitch ends. Trim seam allowance to ⅛" (3 mm). Finger-press the ribbon along the seam.

② Place the wrong sides of ribbon together and stitch ends again from outer edge to inner edge, encasing the raw edges of the ribbon. (This is known as a French seam.) Knot thread, but do not cut.

③ Stitch along the inner edge of the ribbon circle, overlapping one stitch at the end. Pull up on thread, gathering ribbon tightly.

④ Tack to backing. Apply flower center.

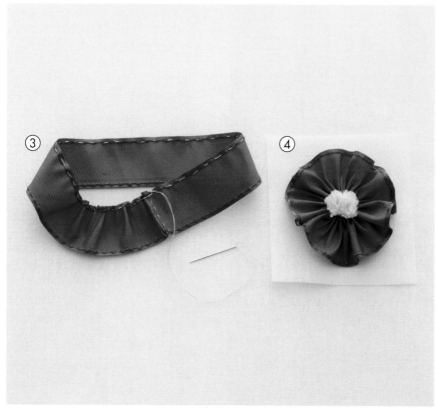

DOUBLE GATHERING LINE

To make buds, berries, or calyxes for stemmed flowers, use the closed method and stitch gathering lines along both edges of the ribbon. Stuff the buds and berries with polyester fiberfill or beads.

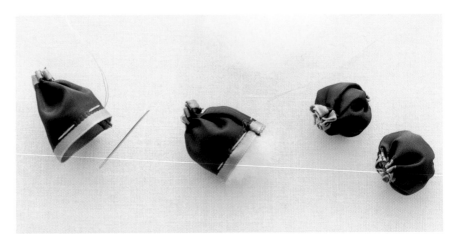

The beautiful colors of pleated silk Shibori ribbon are showcased when a 10" (25.4 cm) length of ribbon is stitched with the closed method, and double gathering lines are sewn along both edges. A Czech pressed glass button is sewn to the center of the ribbon flower.

Gathered Flowers

Rosettes (1): 9 RWs of ⅜" to ⅞" (9 to 23 mm) ribbon; open-end method. Carnations (2): 9 to 11 RWs of ⅝" to 1½" (15 to 39 mm) double-faced ribbon; closed method, running the gathering line slightly off center. After gathering, fold layers so shorter petals are in the middle. Petunia (3): 7 to 9 RWs of 1½" to 2¼" (39 to 56 mm) ribbon; closed method, running a second gathering line ¼ RW away from the first. Gather the edge tight; gather the inner ring around the eraser end of a pencil. Knot. Poppy (4): 4 to 7 RWs per petal layer of 1½" (39 mm) wire-edge ribbon; open-end method for multiple petals. Crimp the outer edge of the petals every ¼" (6 mm) before gathering ribbon. Morning glory (5): 5 RWs of wired ombre ribbon, 1½" (39 mm) wide, closed method.

CONTINUOUS PETAL FLOWERS

Five-petal flowers

① Cut 12½ to 17½ RWs of ribbon, depending on the desired fullness. Remove wire from the inner edge (the edge that is to become the flower center). Apply Fray Check to the ends.

② Mark off five equal sections, 2½ to 3½ RWs wide, along the inner edge. Stitch running stitches in the pattern show, wrapping the thread around the outer edge at each mark.

③ Gather the ribbon tightly. Knot the end to the beginning, turning the raw edges to the back of the flower. Tack the flower to a square of backing. Apply flower center.

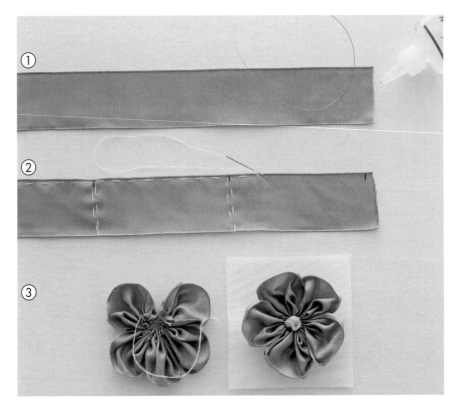

Serpentine gathering

① Mark off both edges of 1½ to 3 yd (1.4 to 2.7 m) of ⅞" or 1½" (23 or 39mm) ribbon into 2-RW segments, staggering the placement on opposite sides by 1 RW.

② Knot thread at the first mark. Stitch diagonally in zigzag pattern, wrapping the thread around the outer edge at each mark.

③ Pull up thread, gathering ribbon to about one-fifth its original length.

④ Form tight circle with first three loops, and tack to backing. Coil the remaining ribbon loosely around the center, tacking inner edges in place as you go. Turn under and tack ribbon end.

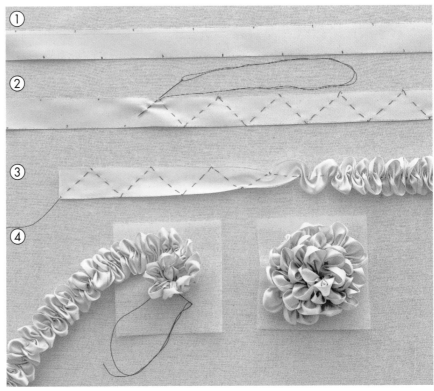

Looped petals

① Mark a ½" (1.3 cm) circle onto backing fabric. Cut 3 yards (2.7 m) of ½" (12 mm) ribbon. Knot the thread near the end of the ribbon.

② Take three small stitches into the ribbon 2" (5 cm) apart, and pull up on thread, forming loops. Tack loops to circle, with loops pointing outward. Repeat, working around the circle.

③ Form an inner layer of loops, as in step 2. Continue to ribbon end. Tack end to backing. Add flower center.

Continuous Petal Flowers

Forget-me-nots (1): ⅝" (15 mm) blue ribbon; tiny pearl button with black bead center. Camellia (2): 50-RW lengths of ⅞" (23 mm) white ribbon; marked off in 3-RW petals, 4-RW petals, and 5-RW petals. Gather and coil with smaller petals in the center. Buttercups (3): ⅞" (23 mm) gold ombre wire-edge ribbon; yellow pompom for the center. Apple blossoms or wild roses (4): ⅝" (15 mm) white or pink ribbon; artificial flower stamens for center. Zinnia (5): 3 to 4 yd (2.7 to 3.7 m) of ³⁄₁₆" (5 mm) grosgrain ribbon; looped petals. Chrysanthemum or aster (6): 3 to 5 yd (2.7 to 4.6 m) of ⅛" (3 mm) satin or grosgrain ribbon; vary the size by varying the loop sizes. Dahlia (7): 3 yd (2.7 m) of 1½" (39 mm) satin ribbon; serpentine-gathered.

Individual Petal Flowers

Form individual petals from short cuts of ribbon, giving them unique shapes by the way you cut the ends or by sewing seams. Then sew them together to make distinctive flowers.

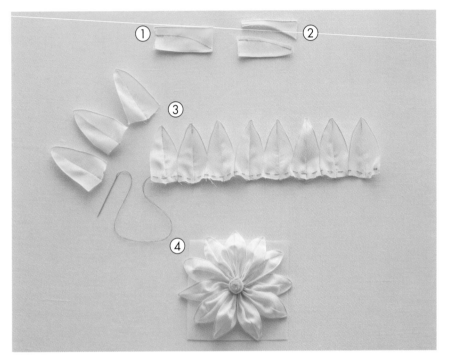

SEAM-SHAPED PETALS

(1) Cut ribbon to desired lengths for individual petals. Fold in half crosswise. Stitch a seam by hand or machine, curving gradually from the petal base to the tip.

(2) Apply Fray Check to both layers ⅛" (3 mm) from the seam; allow to dry. Trim seam allowance to ⅛" (3 mm).

(3) Join petal bases with running stitches; overlap petals slightly for flowers with many single petals. Pull thread to gather, joining petals into a circle.

(4) Tack to backing or secure to stem wire. Apply flower center. Shape petals as desired.

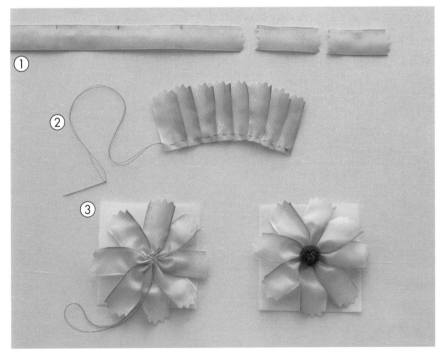

CUT-SHAPED PETALS

(1) Mark off desired petal lengths on ribbon. Apply Fray Check across at each mark and allow to dry. Cut at marks; use pinking shears if desired, or shape petal ends in slight curves.

(2) Join petal bases with running stitches, overlap petals slightly for flowers with many single petals. Pull up thread to gather, joining petals into a circle.

(3) Tack to backing or secure to stem wire. Apply flower center. Shape petals as desired.

Individual Petal Flowers

Dianthus (1): five 1" (2.5cm) lengths of ⅞" (23 mm) white ribbon, cut and shaped with pinking shears, bases tinted red with dye pen. Coneflower (2): ten to fifteen 2" to 4" (5 to 10.2 cm) lengths of pink 1½" (39 mm) wire-edge ribbon seam-shaped; coiled velvet cord center. Daisy (3): Fifteen 3½" (8.9 cm) lengths of ⅞" (23 mm) white/yellow ombre wire-edge ribbon; seam-shaped; frayed grosgrain ribbon center. Black-eyed Susan (4): Fifteen 5" (12.7 cm) lengths of ⅞" (23 mm) gold ombre wire-edge ribbon, seam-shaped; coiled black velvet ribbon center. Coreopsis (5): Eight 1½" (3.8 cm) lengths of ⅝" (15 mm) yellow satin ribbon, cut and shaped with pinking shears, bases tinted with red dye pen. Cosmos (6): Ten 2" (5 cm) lengths of ½" (12 mm) pink ombre ribbon, cut-shaped with curved tips, frayed grosgrain ribbon center. Lily (7): Six 5" to 7" (12.7 to 18 cm) lengths of 1½" or 2¼" (39 or 56 mm) wired ribbon, seam-shaped; artificial stamens. Sword-shaped leaves are also made with the seam-shaped method.

Ribbon Roses

Just as natural roses have many different looks, ribbon roses can be fashioned in various ways. They can be full and ruffly or tailored in tight folds. Make them on long, slender stems with ribbon leaves or stitch them directly to fabric.

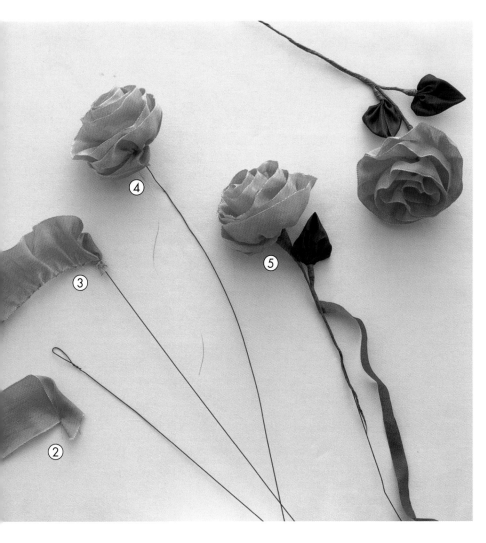

WIRED RIBBON ROSE

① Cut wire-edge ribbon: 16" (40.6 cm) of ⅝" (15 mm); 32" (81.3 cm) of 1½" (39 mm) or 1½ yd (1.4 m) of 2¼" (56 mm). Bend a small loop in the end of a stem wire.

② Pull out about 2" (5 cm) of wire on one edge of one end of ribbon; smooth the ribbon end flat. Fold 2" (5 cm) ribbon end down diagonally, then fold outer edge over. Slip the wire loop inside the folds. Wrap pulled wire around ribbon at bottom of folds, forming rose center.

③ Gather up remaining length of ribbon tightly, sliding ribbon along the same wire from the free end toward the rose center.

④ Wrap gathered edge around rose base, wrapping each layer slightly higher than the previous one. Fold the ribbon ends down and catch under the last layer.

⑤ Wrap ribbon wire tightly around base to secure. Wrap floral tape around rose base, stretching tape and warming it with your fingers for best adhesion. Continue down stem, catching ribbon leaves as you wrap.

For a wired ribbon rose without a stem, omit the stem wire. Stitch the rose center as formed in step 2 to the backing fabric. Work the gathered ribbon around the base, tacking it in place as you go.

TRADITIONAL ROSE (MADE WITH NONWIRED RIBBON)

① Fold 2" (5 cm) ribbon end down diagonally, then fold outer edge over. Slip the wire loop inside the folds. Roll ribbon around base twice.

② Fold ribbon back diagonally. Roll rose center over fold, keeping upper edge of rose center just below upper edge of fold. Roll to end of fold, forming a petal. Wrap tightly with floral wire.

③ Repeat step 2 until rose is desired size. Fold back ribbon end and secure to base. Wrap base with floral tape, continuing down stem wire.

For a traditional rose without a stem, omit stem wire. Stitch the rose center to the backing fabric. Work the ribbon around the base, tacking it in place as you go.

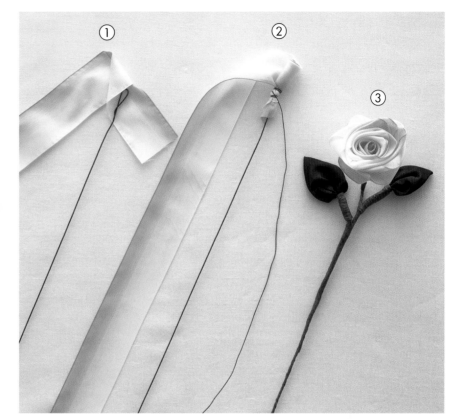

CONCERTINA ROSE

① Cut 12" (30.5 cm) of ⅜" (9 mm) or ½" (12 mm) ribbon. Fold under diagonally at the center, forming a right angle. Turn the end that is underneath back over the center. Repeat with the other side.

② Continue folding alternate ends back over previous folds, forming a square stack. Stop when the ends are 1" (2.5 cm) long.

③ Turn the stack over. Hold only the two ends, and release the stack. Holding ends securely, but loosely enough so they can slide, pull one end gently. A rose will form. Stop pulling when the excess ribbon is pulled out and the center of the rose sinks in. Tack to backing.

Ribbon Roses

Wired ribbon rose wired to stem (1). Wired ribbon roses sewn to backing fabric (2). Traditional rose with leaf, wired to stem (3). Traditional roses sewn to backing fabric (4). Gathered roses made from extra-wide ribbon folded lengthwise; wired to stem or sewn to backing (5). Concertina roses (6).

COMBINATIONS
AND VARIATIONS

Pansy: Five 4-RW lengths of ⅞" (23 mm) to 1½" (39 mm) variegated wire-edge ribbon; two sets of two, overlapped, and gathered into double petals. Gather one piece on the dark side into a single petal. Gathering opposite edges of the double petals heightens contrast and creates the pansy's "face."

Daffodil (1): 1½" (39 mm) gold ombre wire-edge ribbon; 12-RW five-petal base, 6-RW double gathering line center cup. Make base. Gather bottom of cup; tack to base with ⅜" (1 cm) radial stitches outward from center. Add flower stamens. Gather upper edge of cup. Peony (2): 2¼" (56 mm) five-petal base; 3½" (89 mm) rosette center. Canterbury bells (3): 2½ RWs of 1½" (39 mm) ribbon; single gathering line, closed method for flower base; scalloped gathering (page 126) for outer rim of bell.

Leaves

Accent your ribbon flowers with ribbon leaves. Using a few simple shapes, make leaves in all shades of green to complement the flowers and give them a natural-looking setting.

FOLDED LEAF

① Cut a 3-RW length of ribbon. Fold ends down diagonally at the center; fold outer edges in.

② Pleat across the bottom, and twist tightly, if using wire-edge ribbon. Or stitch running stitches across the bottom, catching the lower edge of the back; gather and knot.

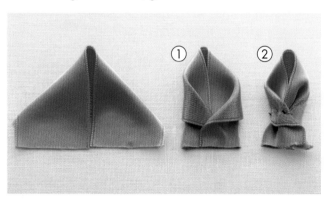

PULLED WIRE LEAF

① Cut 6 RWs of wire-edge ribbon. Pull up on wire from both ends of one side, gathering ribbon evenly toward the center.

② Pleat across the bottom, and twist wire tightly around end. Glue or stitch gathered edges together in center of leaf.

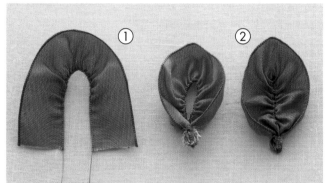

BOAT LEAF

① Cut 6- to 10-RW lengths of ribbon; fold in half crosswise. Fold ends up diagonally, to rest just below upper edge. Pin in place.

② Knot thread at one upper corner. Sew a running stitch down the diagonal fold, across the bottom of the "boat," and up the opposite diagonal fold.

③ Gather to desired fullness; knot. Open leaf and adjust gathers.

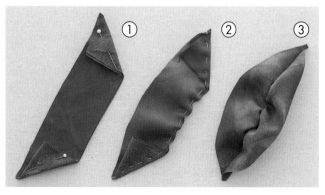

LEAF/CALYX AND STEM

Cut 6- to 10-RW lengths of wire-edge ribbon, depending on desired length of stem. Fold under right angle at center, then fold back over, aligning tails to form pointed leaf or calyx. Twist tails together below leaf to form stem.

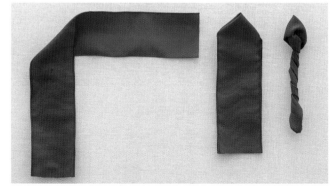

Flower Centers

French knots (1): Use silk ribbon, embroidery floss, or other yarn. Artificial stamens (2): Knot double thread around center of stamen cluster, or wrap floral wire around center, if making flowers with wired stems. Bend cluster in half; secure to flower center. Frayed grosgrain ribbon (3): Cut one selvage from a length of grosgrain ribbon; Remove several rows of threads to fray the edge to within 1/8" (3 mm) of other selvage. Roll from one end; secure to flower center. Ribbon knots (4): Tie a small knot in a short piece of narrow ribbon. Pull tails through flower center, and secure to backing under flower. Coiled chenille stems (5): Hand-tack or glue to flower center. Beaded stamens (6): String bugle beads on fine craft wire for stamen, add seed bead at end, and run wire back down through bugle bead. Repeat for multiple stamens; twist wires together and secure to flower center. Buttons (7): Hand-stitch to flower center, catching seed bead over each hole.

RIBBON EMBROIDERY

Hand embroidery with ribbons, popular at various periods since the eighteenth century, can be used to adorn clothing and personal accessories or to embellish quilts and home décor items. A beautiful piece of ribbon embroidery can be framed and displayed as artwork. A small bit of ribbon embroidery can be used to make a special card or scrapbook page detail.

Soft narrow ribbons, traditionally made from silk, are sewn to a background fabric, using a variety of unique stitches that create graceful curves and delicate raised designs. While some stitches used for ribbon embroidery are similar to those used for embroidering with finer threads, there are special techniques that take advantage of the flat, pliable nature of silk ribbon. Various embroidery threads and beads can be incorporated with silk ribbon to add texture and interest to a design.

Supplies and Preparation

Silk ribbons for embroidery are available in various widths. The most common is 4 mm and you can also find ribbons that are 2 mm, 7 mm, 13 mm, and 32 mm wide. Silk ribbon can be purchased in solid colors as well as variegated and hand-dyed tones. Sheer nylon organdy ribbon also works beautifully for ribbon embroidery.

YOU WILL NEED

- silk ribbons for embroidery
- crewel needles
- tapestry needles
- removable or disappearing marking pens or pencils
- scissors
- embroidery hoop

NEEDLES

The types and sizes of needles needed for ribbon embroidery depend upon the ribbon width, the background fabric, and the stitch. Because these variables change throughout a project, keep on hand an assortment of sharp-pointed crewel needles, sizes 1 to 3, and chenille needles, sizes 18 to 24. The needle eye must be long enough to hold the full width of the ribbon and thick enough to create a hole large enough for the ribbon to easily slide through. Blunt-pointed tapestry needles are useful for stitches that pass between a previous stitch and the fabric, such as spider web roses (page 111) or the wrapping step of a whipped running stitch (page 110).

MARKING METHODS

Embroidery patterns can be transferred to fabric with marking pens and pencils. Because the embroidery may not cover all the marks completely, avoid using permanent markings. Water-soluble or air-soluble markers are useful on light-colored fabrics. Keep in mind that air-soluble marks will disappear in a short period of time. Silver or white quilt marking pencils work well on bright or dark fabrics, and are easily removed or covered.

To transfer the pattern to the fabric, layer the fabric right side up over the pattern and over a light box. A sunny window or a glass-top table with a light placed under it also will work. Or, trace the pattern on sheer netting and transfer the pattern to the fabric through the netting.

PREPARING THE FABRIC

Many fabrics are suitable for ribbon embroidery. The background fabric should be compatible with the look and feel of the design and intended use. Whenever possible, the fabric should be held taut in an embroidery hoop or needlework frame. This prevents the stitches from puckering the fabric, and helps you to develop a consistent stitch tension. To prevent the hoop from imprinting the fabric, wrap the inner hoop with twill tape or yarn.

THREADING AND KNOTTING THE RIBBON

① Thread an 18" (45.7 cm) length of ribbon through the eye of the needle. Pierce the center of the ribbon ¼" (6 mm) from the threaded end; pull the long end of the ribbon, locking the ribbon on the needle eye.

② Fold over the free end of the ribbon ¼" (6 mm), and pierce the center of both layers with the needle. Draw the needle and ribbon through, forming a soft knot at the ribbon end.

Ending

End the ribbon by running the needle to the underside of the fabric; draw the ribbon across the nearest stitch. Piercing both layers, take two small stitches to lock the ribbon. Trim off the ribbon tail.

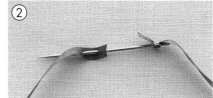

EMBROIDERY WITH NONSILK RIBBONS

Although traditional ribbon embroidery is worked with soft and supple silk ribbon, you can use narrow woven-edge ribbons made from other materials. These ribbons will be thicker and have more body than silk ribbon so the finished look will be a little different. Some of the embroidery stitches shown on the next pages may not work, or will have to be adapted to suit the ribbon and the background.

Look for ribbon that is ¹⁄₁₆" (1.5 mm) to ⅛" (3 mm) wide. Work with short lengths, 18" (45.7 cm) or less, to minimize twisting. If the ribbon does twist while working, drop the threaded needle and allow it to unwind. Then continue to embroider.

Ribbon embroidery stitches can also be sewn onto paper. Lazy daisy stitches (page 110) create the flower accent for this card. Before stitching, pierce holes in the paper where the needle will be inserted.

Stitches

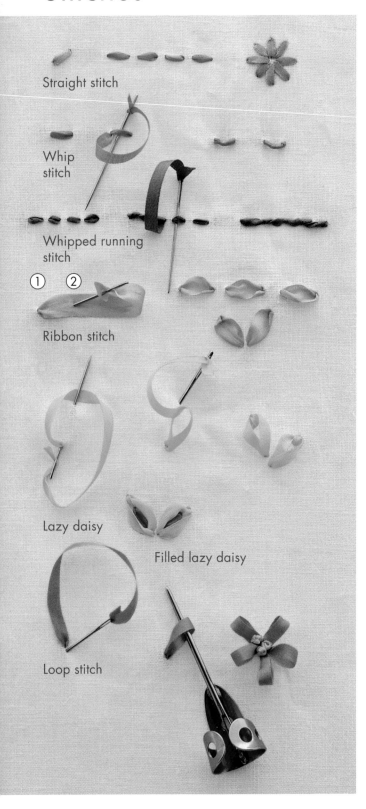

Straight stitch

Whip stitch

Whipped running stitch

① ②

Ribbon stitch

Lazy daisy

Filled lazy daisy

Loop stitch

Straight stitch

Come up at 1 and go down at 2, the desired distance away, keeping the ribbon flat. Make running stitches by continuing in a straight line, with small spaces between the stitches. Make straight stitches that radiate from a single point to create a flower or bud.

Whip stitch

Make a single straight stitch. Bring the needle back up through the fabric at the base of the straight stitch. Wrap the ribbon around the stitch two or three times, keeping the ribbon flat. Go back down in the fabric at the opposite end of the stitch.

Whipped running stitch

Stitch a line of running stitches. Thread ribbon onto a blunt needle. Come up through the fabric at the first stitch. Wrap each stitch twice, keeping the ribbon flat. Proceed to each succeeding stitch to the end of the line before returning to the back of the fabric.

Ribbon stitch

Come up at ①. Smooth the ribbon flat in the direction of the stitch. Insert the needle at the end of the stitch, piercing the center of the ribbon at point ②. Pull the needle through to the underside until the ribbon curls inward at the tip. Take care not to pull the ribbon too tight.

Lazy daisy

Bring the needle up from the underside at the petal base; insert the needle right next to the exit point, and bring the needle back up at the petal tip. Pull the ribbon through the fabric, forming a small, smooth loop. Pass the ribbon over the loop, securing it with a small straight stitch at the tip.

Filled lazy daisy

Make a lazy daisy stitch (see above). Using another color of ribbon, make a straight stitch from the base of the lazy daisy to just below the tip.

Loop stitch

Bring the needle up from the underside, and pull the ribbon through. Loop the ribbon smoothly over a holder, such as a large darning needle. Insert the ribbon needle into the fabric right in front of the exit point. Pull the ribbon through the fabric until the loop tightens around the holder. Continue to hold the completed loop until the next stitch is taken.

Plume stitch

Bring the needle up through the fabric. Stitch back into the fabric, about ⅛" (3 mm) below the first hole. Pull the ribbon through the fabric until the loop tightens around a holder, such as a plastic straw or darning needle held in the nonstitching hand. Bring the needle back up through the fabric, piercing the base of the previous loop. Pull the ribbon through before removing the holder. Repeat to the desired length of the plume.

Stem stitch

Bring the needle up through the fabric at the start of the marked or imaginary stem. Make a small straight stitch. Bring the needle back through the fabric partway back and alongside the previous stitch. Repeat continuously for the desired length, keeping the ribbon smooth without twisting.

Chain stitch

Bring the needle up through the fabric at the beginning of a marked or imaginary line. Form a loop, and insert the needle next to, but not in, the first hole. Bring the needle back out forward on the line, with the needle going over the ribbon. Pull up on the ribbon. Repeat the stitch to the desired line length.

Coral stitch

Bring the needle and ribbon up through the fabric at the starting point. Smooth the ribbon flat along the marked or imaginary line. Make a gentle arch with the ribbon and hold it in place. ①

Take a tiny stitch under the ribbon arch, and pass the needle over the ribbon tail while pulling the ribbon through the fabric. Gradually release the ribbon arch, forming a soft knot. Continue along the line, varying the distance between the knots, flattening or raising segments as desired. ②

Spider web rose

Draw a circle with five evenly spaced spokes. Using embroidery floss or other fine cord, form a stitch along each of the spokes, and tie off. ①

Bring the ribbon up at the center of the web. Weave the ribbon over and under the spokes in a circular fashion, working gradually outward, until the spokes are covered and the desired fullness is achieved. Keep the ribbon loose, as twists in the ribbon add interest. Push the needle through to the back and secure. ②

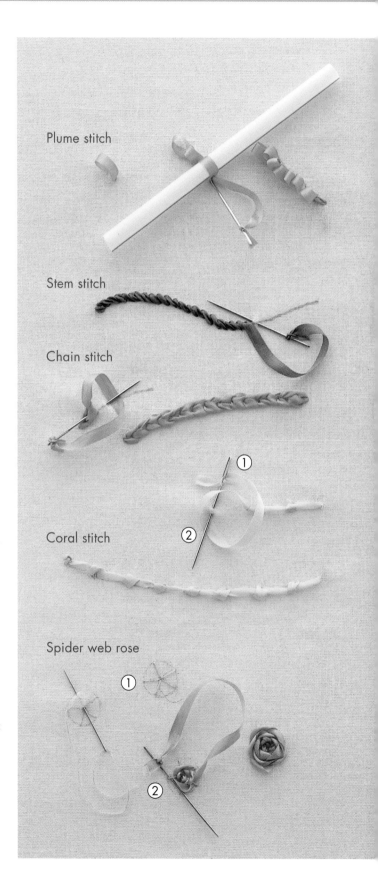

Plume stitch

Stem stitch

Chain stitch

Coral stitch

Spider web rose

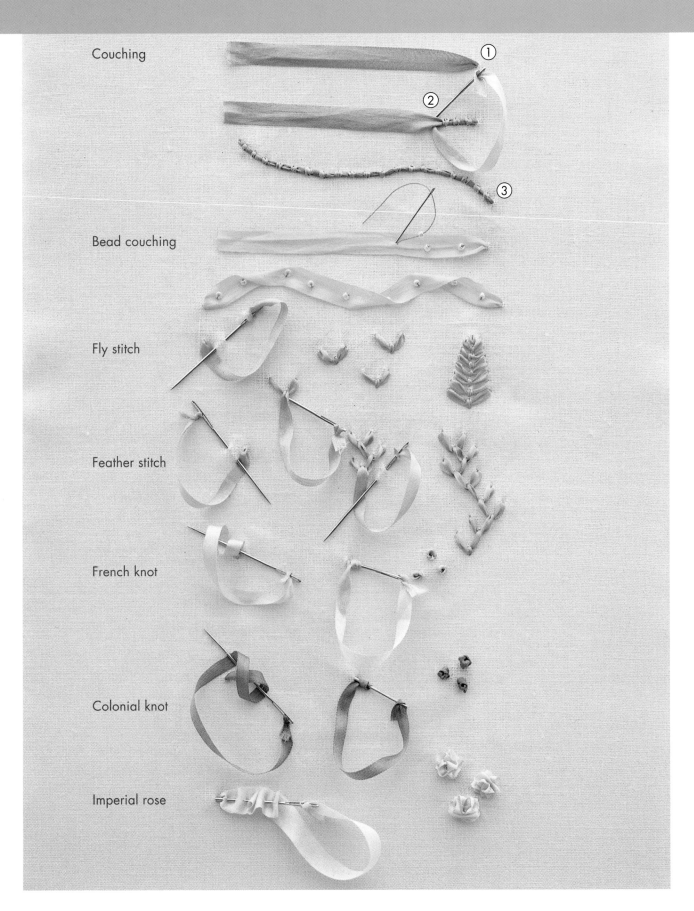

Couching

Bead couching

Fly stitch

Feather stitch

French knot

Colonial knot

Imperial rose

Couching

Thread first needle with ribbon to be couched, then thread second needle with narrower ribbon or thread that will hold the first ribbon in place. Bring first needle up through fabric. Smooth ribbon toward nonstitching hand, and hold under thumb on desired path. ①

Bring second needle up through fabric at first couching point, just below ribbon. Take a small stitch over the wider ribbon. Repeat to end. ②

Pass first needle back through fabric at the end of path, and secure ribbon. Secure couching ribbon or thread at last couching point. ③

Bead couching

Follow directions for couching (above), using beading needle for second needle. Secure seed bead at each couching point. Allow ribbon to twist and turn along line, if desired.

Fly stitch

Bring needle up at 1 and down at 2, keeping ribbon flat and loose. Come up below and halfway between the two points, with the ribbon below the needle. Pull through, forming a V. Insert needle just below point of V to secure. Repeat stitches in a column, narrowing toward the top, to create a stacked fly stitch.

Feather stitch

Follow directions for fly stitch; begin at top of intended line, but don't secure the stitch. Repeat, alternating from left to right. Secure last stitch.

French knot

Bring needle up from underside. Holding needle parallel to fabric near exit point, wrap ribbon once or twice around the needle, taking care to keep the ribbon smooth. Insert needle very close to exit point, holding ribbon in place close to wrapped needle. Hold ribbon while pulling needle through to underside, releasing ribbon as it disappears. Ribbon forms a soft knot.

Colonial knot

Bring needle up through fabric. Form clockwise loop with ribbon, and slide needle tip under it. Then wrap ribbon back over and under the needle in a figure eight. Insert needle back into fabric very near first hole; pull ribbon loosely around needle while drawing needle to back of fabric.

Imperial rose

Bring needle and ribbon up through fabric. Pierce ribbon 1" to 1½" (2.5 to 3.8 cm) above surface; stitch ¼" (6 mm) running stitches in ribbon to just above surface. Insert needle back to underside near first hole. Draw ribbon through gently, stacking folds. Stop when upper fold begins to curl inward.

ROMANTIC RIBBON PILLOW

This romantic pillow, the work of designer Phyllis Dobbs, features a dimensional floral display of silk embroidery around a central wire-edge rose and bow. With its vivid colors and bold design, it would make a lovely addition to a feminine bedroom.

YOU WILL NEED

- 2 yd (1.8 m) fuchsia/pink wire-edge ombre ribbon, ⅞" (23 mm)
- ½ yd (0.5 m) fuchsia satin ribbon, ⅜" (9 mm)
- 1¼ yd (1.2 m) light pink satin ribbon, ⅜" (9 mm)
- periwinkle silk ribbon, 4 mm
- medium pink silk ribbon, 4 mm
- medium green silk ribbon, 4 mm
- light green silk ribbon, 4 mm
- light pink silk ribbon, 7 mm
- ½ yd (0.5 m) cream heavyweight moiré fabric
- 1⅓ yd (1.2 m) cream satin twisted cording
- clear glass seed beads
- polyester fiberfill
- light pink, fuchsia, cream thread
- sewing machine
- hand needle

① Cut out pillow front and back 10½" × 14" (26.9 × 35.6 cm). Transfer pattern to pillow front.

② Fold 1 yd (0.9 m) ombre ribbon into a bow with tails, following the pattern. Hand-sew to pillow front, following pattern.

③ Make a wired ribbon rose (page 100) with the remaining ombre ribbon, gathering along the lighter edge. Stitch the rose to the center of the bow.

④ Make five light pink concertina roses (page 101) and three fuchsia concertina roses. Stitch to pillow front, following pattern. Stitch a clear class bead in the center of each.

⑤ Stitch the lazy daisy leaves, using two shades of green silk ribbon, following the pattern.

⑥ Stitch the lazy daisy flower petals with medium pink silk ribbon. Stitch the loop stitch flowers with 7 mm light pink. Stitch colonial knots in the center of the loop stitch flowers and in the cascading bunches, using the periwinkle ribbon.

⑦ Pin the pillow front to the back, right sides together. Stitch ½" (1.3 cm) seam all around, leaving an opening for turning.

⑧ Turn pillow right side out. Stuff with fiberfill. Whipstitch the cording over the seam line; tuck the ends into the opening, and stitch closed.

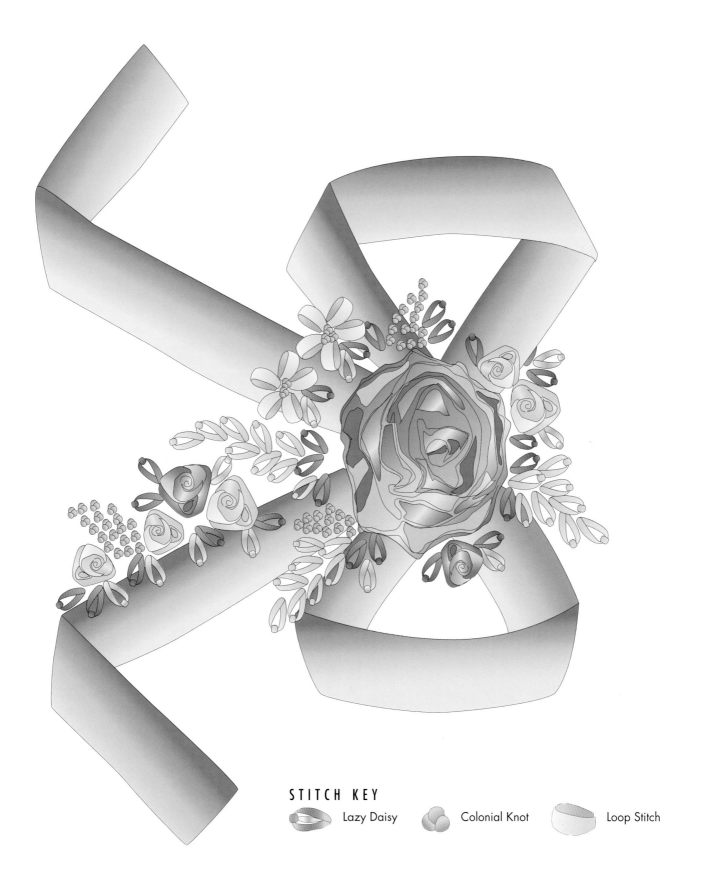

STITCH KEY

Lazy Daisy   Colonial Knot   Loop Stitch

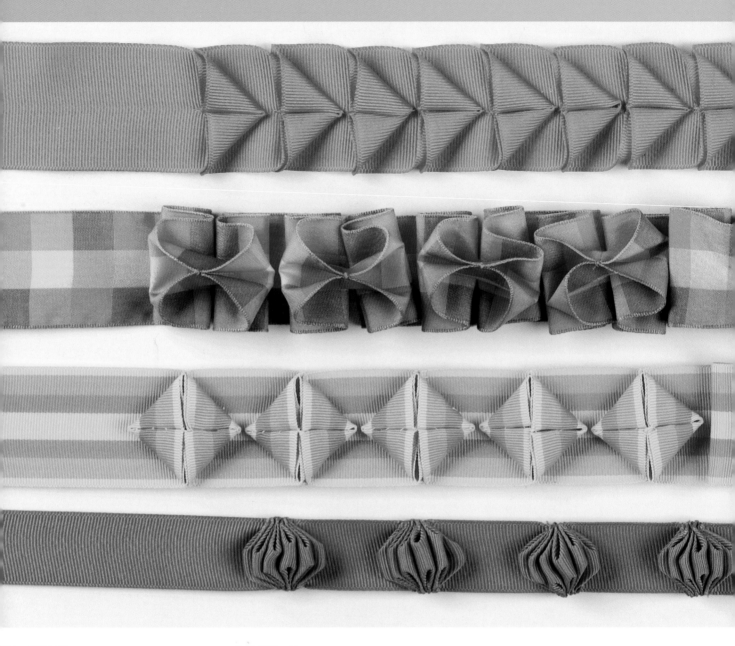

RIBBON TRIMS, ROSETTES
AND TASSELS

Ribbons have long been used to create interesting embellishments. Victorian fashion books often featured involved trims and millinery adornments constructed from ribbons that had been braided, pleated, folded, gathered, smocked, and manipulated in complicated ways. Although the types and colors of ribbons available today make it easy to embellish projects with just a simple row of ribbon, it is fun to explore these vintage techniques to make a unique detail to add to a special craft or sewing project.

Braided Ribbon Trims

Braiding with ribbon makes interesting patterned trims that are flexible and can be shaped into gentle curves when necessary. This makes them especially appropriate for trimming garments, accessories, and projects for the home. A wide multicolor braid makes a great belt, and a petite satin braid becomes a charming finish for the edge of a bride's shoes. Braids of various styles and sizes are perfect for headbands and barrettes or home décor items such as napkin rings, lampshade edgings, or drapery tieback accents.

A padded surface, such as a covered ironing board, is helpful for most braiding techniques, as the ribbon ends can be secured with pins, leaving both hands free to braid. Ribbons up to 7/8" (23 mm) wide can be braided successfully; however, flat multi-ply braiding is most successful with narrower ribbons, especially grosgrains. Rolled braiding and loop braiding expose both sides of the ribbon, which can create interesting effects with single-faced ribbons. Finish the ends of braided trims by turning the raw edges back and hand-tacking. To form a circle with the finished braid, stitch the ends together and hide raw edges on the inside.

Rolled three-ply braids are used for the spaghetti straps of this gown. Two-tone braids crisscross at the back and cascade down creating streamers of picot-edge and plain satin ribbon.

FLAT THREE-PLY BRAID

Cut three ribbons about one-sixth longer than desired finished length of trim. Pin ribbons side by side on padded pinning surface. Pass the left ribbon over the middle ribbon, then the right ribbon over the middle, continuing in this pattern. Always keep the ribbon facing up and relatively flat.

ROLLED THREE-PLY BRAID

As above, pin ribbons side-by-side to surface. Roll the left ribbon over the middle, then the right over the middle, continuing in this pattern. Keep even tension on all three ribbons; the outer edges will form straight lines.

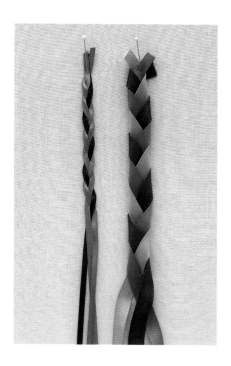

ROLLED FOUR-PLY BRAID

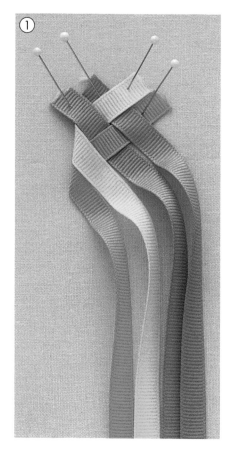

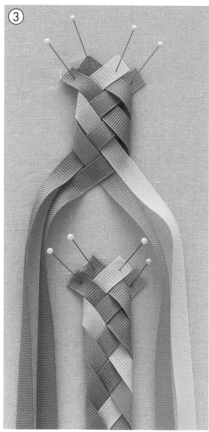

① Cut four ribbons about one-third longer than desired finished length of trim. Pin ribbons in sets of two at right angles to each other; weave them together as shown. Roll the two left ribbons to the right at right angles.

② Roll the far right ribbon under the adjacent ribbon, over the next, and under the last. Repeat with the ribbon that is now on the far right.

③ Roll the two left ribbons to the right at right angles. Repeat step 2. Continue in this pattern to the desired length.

FIVE-PLY BRAID

Cut five ribbons around one-sixth longer than desired finished length of trim. Pin ribbons side by side on surface. Weave the outer right ribbon over and under the other ribbons until it becomes the outer left ribbon. Repeat with ribbon that has shifted to the outer right. Continue this pattern to the desired length.

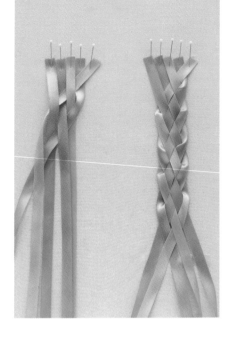

SINGLE RIBBON LOOP BRAID

Select a ribbon that is double-faced, as the wrong side of the ribbon will show with this braiding technique. Depending upon the width of ribbon, you will need up to nine times the desired finished length of the braid.

① Hold the ribbon at the center and form a flat loop by crossing the right ribbon over the left. With the ribbon coming from the top of the cross, create another flat loop by folding the ribbon back on itself, wrong sides together, and slipping it into the previous loop.

② Draw the loops together snugly, down to the ribbon width.

③ Pick up the ribbon on the right side; fold it back on itself to make a flat loop and slit it through the left loop. Draw the left loop snug.

①
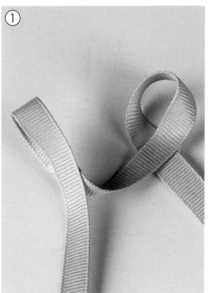

②

③

④ Form a flat loop with the ribbon on the left side and slip it through the right loop. Draw the right loop snug. Continue to follow this pattern to the desired finished length.

⑤ When the braid is the desired length, pull the end of the ribbon all the way through the last loop and cut both ribbons at a length equal to the width of the ribbon. Tuck these tabs under and tack them down with a needle and thread.

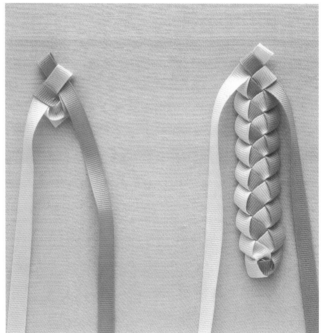

Variations

For an interesting effect, use a double-sided ribbon with different colors on each side, or hold two colors of the same width ribbon together and braid them as one.

Cut two coordinating ribbons, each four to five times longer than the desired finished length of the braid. Use a needle and thread to hand-tack a loop at the end of each ribbon, creating an opening equal to the ribbon width. Hold one ribbon in each hand and slip the left loop through the right loop. Braid the ribbons, following the directions above for the single ribbon loop braid.

Pleated and Folded Ribbon Trims

Ribbons can be pleated, folded, manipulated, and sewn to create a variety of special effects. Often one edge of a pleated trim is stitched in place and the pleats along the free edge fan out slightly. In some applications, the trim may be stitched down the center, allowing both free edges to fan out. Because pleated trims are fairly flexible, they can be used around some curves. Closely spaced or stacked pleats, sewn along one edge, offer the most flexibility.

Knife pleats and box pleats are the bases for more detailed trims that involve repetitive folding, rolling, and hand-tacking. Ribbons of all sizes and types can be used, keeping in mind that the detailed trims may reveal both sides of the ribbon. Wire-edge ribbons can be used, although it may be necessary to remove the wires to reduce bulk. Striped ribbons can add an unexpected pattern when formed into a pleated or folded trim.

To make the instructions universal for any width of ribbon, measurements are given in reference to ribbon widths (RWs). The chart below will help you determine the total amount of ribbon necessary for trims that have evenly spaced and stacked knife and box pleats. For other styles, short test samples are the best way to estimate yardage needed for the desired finished length of trim.

YOU WILL NEED

- ribbon
- air-soluble marking pen
- scissors
- hand needle and thread
- sewing machine (optional)

PLEATING STYLE	RIBBON LENGTH NEEDED
Single knife or box pleats	3 times the finished length
Double knife or box pleats	5 times the finished length
Triple knife or box pleats	7 times the finished length

KNIFE PLEATS

Knife pleats are folded with all the pleats going in the same direction.

① Using an air-soluble marking pen, place marks one ribbon width (1 RW) apart along one edge of the ribbon. Fold in single, double, or triple knife pleats. Hand-stitch along one edge or down the center of the ribbon.

② Fold the next pleat or set of pleats 1 RW from the last fold. Continue this pattern to the desired length. Turn under and stitch the end, if it will not be hidden in a seam.

The top ribbon trim is a single knife pleat, hand-stitched along the edge. The bottom ribbon trim is a double knife pleat with machine stitching down the center. If machine stitching, fold pleats toward you and stop stitching with the needle down one or two stitches into the pleat. Fold the next pleat or set of pleats and continue to stitch.

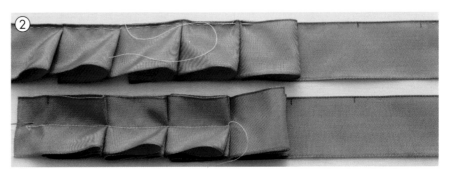

BOX PLEATS

Box pleats are folded with the under edges toward the center

of each pleat, creating a box shape on the front.

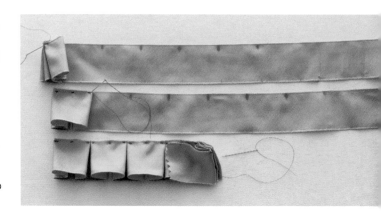

① Using an air-soluble marking pen, place marks one ribbon width apart along one edge of the ribbon. For a single box pleat, fold a stack of two pleats, ½ RW, folding the ribbon tail back over the stack. For a double box pleat, fold a stack of four pleats, ½ RW wide, folding the ribbon tail back over the stack. Hand-tack along one edge or at the center of the folds, taking a tiny stitch into each of the folds.

② Open the fold into a box pleat. Hand-tack the outer edges of the folds in place at the edge or center.

③ Fold consecutive box pleats so that the folds touch. Or skip a ½ RW between the folds. Stitch continuously.

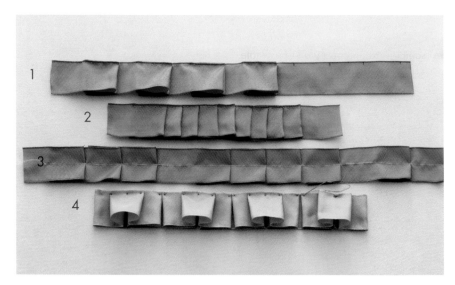

Create different looks by varying the size and spacing of the pleats and the position at which they are stitched.

Double 1-RW knife pleats, ½ RW between (1).

Single 1-RW knife pleats, overlapping ½ RW (2).

Clustered 1-RW knife pleats; clusters separated by 1 RW (3).

Double box pleats made with 1-RW and ½-RW folds (4).

A Perfect Pleater makes it quick and easy to create knife pleated ribbon—without having to do any markings. Follow the manufacturer's instructions and tuck the ribbon into the louvers of the pleater. Use a damp press cloth and iron to set the pleats. Allow the pleats to cool before removing the ribbon from the pleater. You can make continuous pleats by repeating the pleating process along the length of the ribbon. Secure the pleats by sewing along the side or down the center or applying wash-away tape. Different size pleats can be made by using every other or every third louver. Unstitched pleated ribbon can be used to make beautiful bows and ribbon flowers.

PLEATED AND FOLDED TRIM VARIATIONS

Flying geese

Use a ribbon that's approximately three times the length of the finished trim. Make center-tacked ½-RW knife pleats. Fold the outer corners to the center, forming a triangle and tack in place. Repeat so the point of each triangle touches the base of the adjacent one.

Pulled box pleats

The ribbon for this pleated and ruffled trim needs to be about four times the length of the finished trim. The box pleats can be sewn by machine and finished by hand. Make center-stitched single or double box pleats, 1 RW wide. Pull the top selvages together at the center of each pleat and hand-tack. A small bead can be sewn to each center point, if desired.

Diamonds and squares

The striped ribbon used for this sample creates an interesting geometric pattern. Use a ribbon that is about three times the length of the finished trim. Make box pleats just a bit less than 1 RW wide. Fold the two outer corners of the left side of each pleat to the center and tack. Repeat with the right side corners of each pleat.

Paddlewheels

Use a ribbon that is approximately six times the length of the finished trim. Fold a stack of six ½-RW pleats. On the wrong side, just inside each selvage, hand-stitch the pleats together. Flatten the base ribbon and fan out the pleats. Tuck both sides of each pleat into the center. (You may find it helpful to use a pin or the tip of your scissors to fold the ribbon into the pleat.) From the back side, stitch through all folds near the edges of the base ribbon. Space the paddlewheels evenly down the ribbon. The size and number of the pleats, as well as the spacing between the paddlewheels can vary.

An individual paddlewheel motif can be made by folding a length of ribbon with enough pleats to create a complete circle. This ornament was made from 1¼ yards (1.2 m) of 2¼" (56 mm) striped grosgrain ribbon. Eighteen 1⅛" (2.9 cm) pleats were folded and tacked at the top and bottom to form the circle. The ends of each pleat were tucked into the center of the pleats, forming the ornament shape. One-half yard (0.5 m) of ⅝" (15 mm) ribbon is knotted together near the ends and inserted through the center of the ornament. The knot is stitched to the bottom of the ornament and the loop creates the hanger for attaching the ornament to the tree.

Bows-in-a-row

Tiny bows are pleated down the length for this ribbon trim. You will need about three times the length of the finished trim. For each bow, make a knife pleat that is two-thirds the ribbon width and stitch across the width of the ribbon. Fold the loop just made into three even pleats and tack together at the center on the right side of the ribbon. Spread the pleats at the edges and tack the corners of the outer pleats to the base. The corners will not reach all the way to the edge of the base but will curve in a bit. Leave ½ RW between bows.

Bow ties

The double-faced brown/sage ribbon used for this sample adds a distinctive contrast to the folds of this pleated and stitched trim. Use a ribbon that is approximately three times the length of the finished trim. Make single box pleats 2 RWs wide. Overlap the top selvages at the center of each pleat and secure with a bead, button, or small ribbon flower. The bows can be placed next to each other or spaced farther apart.

Zigzag

This trim is made by folding and twisting the ribbon in an alternating diagonal repeat. You will need about one-and-one-third times the length of the finished trim. Make folds in the ribbon as shown. The width of the base of each triangle is 1 RW. Always twist the ribbon in the same direction. Tack the folds where the ribbon edges met.

Although each side of this trim is different, either one or both can be used on a project.

Prairie points

Like the prairie points made from fabric, ribbon can be easily folded to create this trim. Use about one-and-one-third times the length of the finished trim. The ribbon is folded into a diagonal repeat as shown for the zigzag trim. The ribbon twists in one direction for one set of folds, and in the opposite direction for the alternating set. Tack the folds where the ribbon edges meet. Fold every other point up along the center of the trim so all the tips point in the same direction.

Gathered Ribbon Trims

Gathering ribbon is known as ruching. Softly ruffled and bubbled ribbon trims can be made with patterns of running stitches. Some of the gathering stitches can be sewn by machine, especially for wider ribbons. Consistent stitch length and spacing is important; multiples and fractions of ribbon widths are used for spacing. Longer stitches result in tighter, deeper gathers; shorter stitches in looser, shallower gathers. Wire-edge ribbons can be gathered simply by pulling the wire along one edge. The wires can also be removed and the edges sewn with ¼" (6 mm) running stitches.

Smocking pulls the ribbon into soft ripples in a repeated design, by pulling together and knotting groups of strategically placed stitches. The stitches are hidden on the back side of the ribbon, and only the pulled design shows on the front.

Soft, supple ribbons are best to use for ruched manipulation techniques. Because the amount of ribbon taken up varies with the length of the running stitches and the tightness to which the gathers are pulled, work directly from the ribbon spool whenever possible or measure test samples to estimate the length needed.

STRAIGHT-LINE GATHERING

Hand- or machine-stitch running stitches along one edge or down the center of the ribbon. For a layered ruffle effect, place narrow ribbon on top of wide ribbon; stitch and gather them together. Stitch multiple rows for a shirred look. Longer stitches produce tighter gathers.

Wires removed from wire-edge ribbon; gathered on one edge with long hand stitches (1)
Wires removed; gathered on short hand stitches (2)
Machine-gathered down the center (3)
Layered ribbons and gathered (4)
Machine-gathered; three rows (5)

PATTERNED GATHERING

Stitch running stitches in a marked pattern. Gather the ribbon to the desired fullness; arranging it evenly along the thread.

Serpentine (1): Marks are 2 RWs apart on each edge and staggered; wrap thread around selvage at each turn.
Shell (2): Marks are 1 RW apart; wrap thread around selvage at points.
Scallop (3): Marks are ½ RW apart; stitch zigzags ¼ RW in from edge.

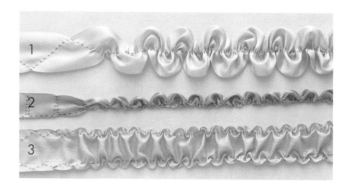

SHELL SMOCKING

Shell smocking is suitable for narrower ribbons, up to 1½" (39 mm) wide.

① Mark off both edges in 1-RW spaces. Mark center of ribbon halfway between each set of outer marks.

② Knot thread at first outer edge mark. Take a small stitch in first center mark and another in opposite outer mark. Pull the three points together and knot.

③ Knot thread at the next outer mark, allowing it to lie flat between knots.

④ Repeat steps 2 and 3 down the ribbon to the desired length.

LATTICE SMOCKING

Lattice smocking is most effective on wider ribbons where at least two rows of smocking can be worked.

① Cut ribbon slightly longer than 1¼ times the desired finished length of the trim. Mark a grid of dots ¼" (6 mm) apart, centered on ribbon back, with an odd number of dots across.

② Knot thread at dot 1. Take a small stitch at dot 2; pull 1 and 2 together and knot. Knot thread at dot 3, allowing it to lie flat between knots. Take a small stitch at dot 4; pull 3 and 4 together and knot.

③ Continue this pattern, working from side to side down the length of the ribbon. Note that every other dot to the left and right of the column will be skipped.

④ Work the second column, following steps 2 and 3, beginning with dot 5, and taking stitches at dots that were omitted along right side of first column. Work remaining columns.

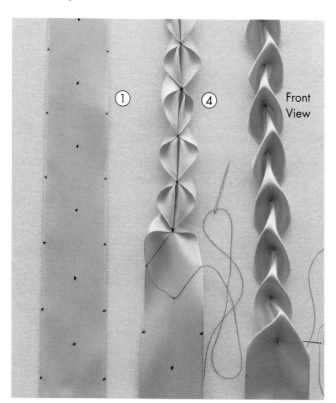

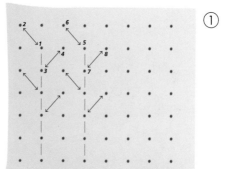

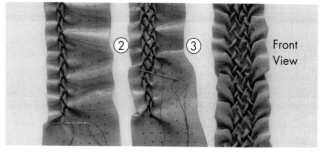

GATHERED TRIM VARIATIONS

Gathers and spaces

This trim looks best when worked with narrow ribbon. The sample shown is made with ⅝" (15 mm) double-faced satin. You will need about four times the length of the finished trim. For a distance of 3 RWs, work a line of running stitching lengthwise down the center of the ribbon. Pull thread to gather; knot and cut thread. Move 1½ RWs along the ribbon and repeat. Twist the gathers neatly into an S shape.

Ribbon beads

Use approximately 1¼ times the length of the finished trim. This trim can be stitched by hand or machine. Work running stitches across the width of the ribbon. Pull on the thread to gather the ribbon tightly; knot and cut thread. Move 1 RW along the ribbon and repeat. The gathered ribbon beads can be stuffed with batting, cotton balls, or a large bead. The gathers can be covered with small beads or wrapped with decorative cording.

Semicircles

You will need a length of ribbon three times the desired length of the finished trim. This trim can be machine- or hand-stitched. Work short running stitches along one selvage edge for 3 RWs. Pull thread to gather tightly; knot and cut thread. Insert needle into opposite edge, at the same point as the last stitch on the opposite side. Work stitching along this selvage edge for 3 RWs. Gather tightly; knot and cut thread. Repeat the pattern, alternating stitching along the selvages from side to side. The ribbon will curve into an S shape.

Fold every other semicircle to one side to create a ruffled edging trim.

Circles and dots

Approximately one-and-one-half times the length of the finished trim will be used. The large printed circles on the ribbon used for this sample make it easy to create this trim. For a solid ribbon, create a circle pattern about ¼" (6 mm) smaller than the ribbon width. Mark the center of each circle every 2 RWs along the ribbon and trace the outlines of the circle pattern onto the back of the ribbon. Stitch along the circle edge with small running stitches. Pull to gather. If desired, stuff the dot with batting. Tighten stitches; knot and cut thread. Repeat down the ribbon.

Corded gathers

Depending upon the ribbon selected, you will need one-and-one-half to three times the length of the finished trim. Cut a length of narrow cording the same length as the ribbon. Fold the ribbon in half lengthwise, wrong sides together, around the cording. Stitch the cord to the ribbon at one end. Machine-stitch close to the cording, using a zipper foot. Be careful not to catch the cording in the stitching. Press the flat edges of the ribbon open. Pull on the cording to gather the ribbon. Stitch the end of the ribbon to the cording; trim excess cording. Adjust gathers evenly down the length of the trim.

Wrapped candy

Gathered flutes along a wide ribbon look like wrapped candies. You will need about three times the length of the finished trim. If you are using a striped or plaid ribbon, you can follow the lines for placement of the flutes. For a solid ribbon, fold the ribbon into a ¼-RW knife pleat and stitch across the width, starting and ending the stitching about ¼ RW from each edge. Knot thread and cut. Finger-press the pleat into a cylinder. Stitch and gather both ends of the flute. Repeat down the ribbon.

Ribbon Rosettes

In years past, circles of elaborate ribbon trims, known as rosettes or cockades, were worn as badges of honor on a hat or lapel. The colors of the ribbon often showed the wearer's allegiance to a political organization or rank. In the early 1900s, instructions were available to make ribbon "fancies" to decorate your frock or hat. And who has not valued the coveted "blue ribbon" for winning a horse race or spelling bee?

Today ribbon rosettes can add flair to the home by accenting a picture on the wall or the ends of a neckroll pillow. Ribbon rosettes can be used to make prize ribbons for any contest or to commemorate a special occasion: happy birthday, bride-to-be, new baby, etc. Any day can be made memorable by awarding a prize ribbon to a special sister or a friend who is young at heart. Ribbon rosettes can decorate a handbag, embellish a card, or be worn as jewelry. It is fun to think of contemporary ways to use these vintage embellishments.

Traditionally, ribbon rosettes were constructed and sewn to crinoline (a crisp fabric used to stiffen hats or make petticoats) or buckram (coarse material, sized with glue, used in bookmaking and garment-making). You can also form ribbon rosettes on stiff interfacing or felt, or glue them together on cardstock or chipboard.

GATHERED RIBBON ROSETTE

It is easy to gather a ribbon circle and create a ruffled rosette. Wire-edge ribbon can be used by removing the wire along one edge and using the remaining wire to gather. For a fuller rosette, it is best to remove both wires and use hand stitches to gather the rosette in the center.

① Form ribbon into a circle, right sides together, and stitch cut ends. If the rosette is to be used on a garment that may be washed, you may want to enclose the raw edges of the ribbon as described on p. 93 for ribbon flower closed gathering method.

② Stitch running stitches along one edge of the ribbon.

③ Pull thread to gather; knot and cut thread.

RIBBON MEDALLION

An accordion-pleated length of ribbon is stitched into a circle and shaped to create this pinwheel medallion. The sample is made with grosgrain ribbon pressed in sharp folds. The same technique can be used with satin or sheer ribbon and not pressed so that the folds are soft and ruffled.

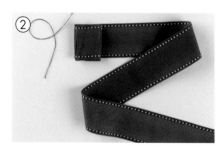

YOU WILL NEED

- 1 yd (0.9 m) of 1½" (39 mm) ribbon
- needle and thread
- pins

① Thread the needle with a doubled length of thread and knot; set aside.

② Fold one end of the ribbon down 1" (2.5 cm). Accordion-pleat the length of the ribbon by folding the ribbon back and forth, making sure all the pleats are 1" (2.5 cm) wide. Hold the folds together as you make the pleats. Finish the pleating with the remaining end of the ribbon facing the same direction as the beginning end.

③ Trim excess ribbon. Bring needle back into the first pleat, creating a circle. Do not knot thread. Let threaded needle hang from the center of the circle.

④ Place medallion on ironing board or pinable surface. Evenly space and overlap the outer edges of the medallion, and pin each to hold. The center edges of the pleats should form a spiral pattern. Pull up on threaded needle to tighten. When the pleats are evenly spaced, the center of the medallion, or the entire medallion, can be pressed. Carefully unpin and secure the center folds from the back with a few stitches to close any opening at the center. Slipstitch the cut edges of the ribbon together.

RIBBON WHEEL ROSETTE

The ribbon wheel rosette looks similar to the medallion rosette, but the loops are made from individual lengths of ribbon. Unlike the medallion, which is made from one length of ribbon, the ribbon wheel can be made from two or more coordinating ribbon colors and patterns. A ribbon-covered or matching shank button is sewn at the center to cover the raw ends of the ribbon loops.

YOU WILL NEED

- 1 yd (0.9 m) of ribbon (if using two colors, you will need ½ yd [0.5 m] of each)
- square of 1½" (39 mm) ribbon.
- 1¾" (4.5 cm) circle of stiff felt
- needle and thread
- ⅞" (2.2 cm) covered button kit

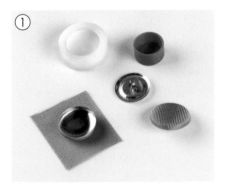

① Follow manufacturer's instructions to cover the button.

② Cut ribbon into twelve 3" (7.6 cm) lengths. If you are using two colors, cut six lengths of each color.

③ Fold each ribbon length in half. Hold them together with a stitch at the center of the raw edges. Alternating color, position and stitch the loops to the circle. Make sure that the beginning loop overlaps the final loop.

④ Sew the button to the center of the rosette. From the back, slipstitch one layer of each ribbon loop to edge of the felt circle.

PETAL ROSETTE

Like the wheel rosette, the petal rosette is made with individual ribbon lengths. The ribbons are folded into petal shapes and attached around a base of stiff felt or cardboard. The center can be filled with any type of smaller rosette. The sample shown has a gathered rosette made from 1½" (39 mm) ribbon and a ⅞" (23 mm) ribbon-covered button at the center. Double-sided satin ribbon is formed into a loop with tails (see Ribbons for a Cause, page 8). The finished rosette is glued onto the loop at the point where the ribbons overlap.

YOU WILL NEED

- 60" (1.7 m) of ⅞" (23 mm) ribbon for the petals
- 3" (7.6 cm) circle of stiff felt
- fusible web
- needle and thread or glue

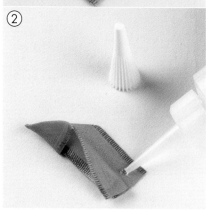

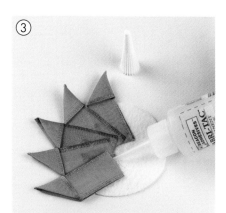

① Cut twelve 5" (12.7 cm) length of ribbon. At the center point of each length, fold ends down, creating a triangle shape. Press.

② Fold the triangle in half, placing ribbon tails on top of each other and press. Secure the base of each petal with fusible web, stitches, or glue.

③ Position petals around the circle base, creating a spiral shape. Make sure that all the petals are going in the same direction. Fuse, stitch, or glue petals to base.

④ Add center rosette and tails, if desired. If ribbon tails are added, a circle of coordinating felt can be glued to the back of the base.

PLEATED RIBBON ROSETTE

This is the classic prize ribbon rosette—pleated ribbon spiraled into a circle. You can use any type of ribbon. It can be constructed by gluing the pleated ribbon to a cardboard circle or sewing it to a stiff felt or interfacing circle. The center can be filled with a covered button, chipboard circle, or any other embellishment or small ribbon rosette.

① Fold back the cut edge of one end of the ribbon ¼" (6 mm) and pin. Make a ¼" (6 mm)-wide angled knife pleat every ½" (1.3 cm) on the right side of the ribbon and pin each pleat. (It is not necessary to mark the ribbon, just use your eye to gauge the pleats about the same size and distance apart.) As you move along the length of the ribbon, you will start to see it spiral. Continue to pleat the entire ribbon length. Fold back the remaining cut edge of the ribbon ¼" (6 mm) and pin.

② Machine-stitch a straight stitch along the inner side of the spiraled ribbon to secure the pleats at the very edge. Remember to remove the pins as you sew.

③ Begin to wrap the pleated ribbon into a spiral. It can be secured to the cardboard circle with glue or sewn by hand to the felt circle. Continue to spiral the ribbon around the circle, placing each row slightly more into the center of the circle so that about ⅜" (1 cm) of the previous row of pleats shows.

④ Glue or sew a button or embellishment to the center. If desired, add ribbon tails to the back. Sew or glue the finished rosette to your project or cover the back of the rosette with another paper or felt circle if you are using it as a prize pin.

YOU WILL NEED

- 2 yd (1.8 m) of ⅞" (23 mm) ribbon

- straight pins

- 3" (7.6 m) circle of cardboard or felt.

- sewing machine to stitch pleats (although they can also be done by hand)

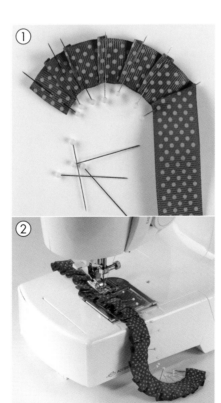

Wire-edge pleated ribbon rosette variation

Wire-edge ribbons will keep their folds when pleated and do not need to be sewn to hold them together. For consistently even pleats, follow the directions on page 123 for pleating ribbon with the Perfect Pleater. The rosette shown was made with two rows of pleated ribbons with a double gathered rosette in the center. A ribbon flower could also be used as the center.

FOLDED RIBBON BUTTON

This six-sided folded ribbon button can be used at the center of a larger rosette or it can be used as an embellishment itself. The striped ribbon used on the sample shown adds additional interest to the lines of the folds. An accent button can be sewn to the center of the ribbon button, and ribbon streamers can be added.

YOU WILL NEED

- ½ yd (0.5 m) of ⅞" (23 mm) ribbon (if you select a wider ribbon, you will need more length)
- needle and thread
- pins

① Fold ribbon at a 60 degree angle at the center.

② Bring the right-hand ribbon over the left and pin.

③ Rotate the point created to the left a little and bring the right ribbon over the left; pin.

(continued)

④ Rotate the points again and bring the right ribbon over the left; pin.

⑤ Rotate and bring the right ribbon over the left; pin. To assure that the button is symmetrical, the edge of the ribbon on this turn should be parallel to the edge of the first fold.

⑥ Repeat folding pattern two more times. Slip ribbon tails under first point. Trim excess ribbons and hand-tack layers to secure.

④

⑤

⑥

STAR POINT ROSETTE

A series of overlapping folded triangles create the star points for this ribbon rosette. A small star point rosette can be used in the center of a larger gathered or pleated rosette. The striped grosgrain ribbon used for the sample shown adds interest to the shape of the finished rosette. The inside points of the star can be sewn together and slightly twisted before a button is sewn to the center.

①

②

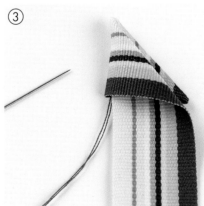

③

YOU WILL NEED

- ½ yd (0.5 m) of ⅞" (23 mm) ribbon (If using a wider ribbon, you will need more length and will have to fold more star points.)

- needle and thread

① At one end of the ribbon, turn the edge under ¼" (6 mm) and press to the wrong side. With the wrong side up and the finished edge to the right, fold the upper right corner down to the lower edge of the ribbon. Sew the pressed end to the long side of the ribbon.

② With the working end of the ribbon to the left, fold ribbon down to form a triangle. Leave a small space between the ribbon edges. This gap allows for the fold of the ribbon.

③ Fold the triangle in half with the gap as the center; align the diagonal folds. One full point has been made.

④ Make another point by folding the ribbon to the left and leaving a small gap between the ribbon edges.

⑤ Fold up the lower half using the gap as the center; align the diagonal folds. Whipstitch through the inside corner of the triangle. Leave the threaded needle hanging.

⑥ Fold the ribbon down, making another point. Continue folding until you have nine points, ending with the ribbon folded as in step 2. Turn under raw edges and secure with small stitches. Pull the stitches and adjust. Make a circle by joining the ends and secure with a few stitches.

⑦ Stitch together the inside top points of the rosette and pull tight to close the center. If desired, a button can be stitched to the center of the rosette.

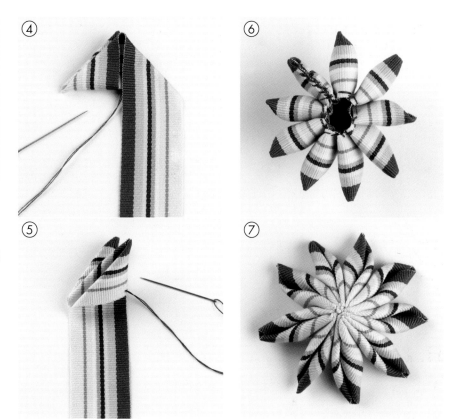

Star point rosette with loops

This variation of the basic star point rosette is made with 2 yards (1.8 m) of 1½" (39 mm) ribbon. Twenty-one points are folded, following the instructions above. The points of the finished rosette are stitched down to a 3" (7.6 cm) circle of stiff felt. Each outer loop is made from 2" (5 cm) of ⅝" (15 mm) ribbon, folded in half, and inserted between the points. The loops are stitched to the felt base, and a button is added to the center of the rosette.

Ribbon Tassels

Like the familiar ornament that swings from a mortar board on graduation day, tassels are eye-catching and add a touch of color and movement to a decorating project or gift. Tassels can be made from a wide variety of materials, including ribbons. They are fun to make and are great decorating accents hanging from an antique key, attached to the corners of a pillow or drapery tiebacks, or hanging from a light pull. A tassel can be made entirely with ribbons, or ribbons can be combined with coordinating yarns, threads, and trims. Combining narrow ribbon remnants to make a tassel is a nice way to use ribbon leftovers from other projects.

The main components of a tassel are the cord or hanger, the head, the neck, and the body or skirt. Elaborate tassels can be made by using wood tassel forms for the head, wrapping the neck with decorative trims and small ribbon roses, and adding many layers of overskirts to the body.

YOU WILL NEED

- The amount of ribbon needed to make a basic tassel will depend upon the desired finished length and fullness of the tassel. The following list is for the tassels shown.

- 4½ to 7 yd (4.1 to 6.4 m) of ⅛" (3 mm) to ⅜" (9 mm) ribbon

- floral wire

- glue or needle and thread

BASIC RIBBON TASSEL

The basic ribbon tassel is made by wrapping ribbon around a piece of cardboard. The size of the cardboard and the number of times the ribbon is wrapped will determine the finished size of the tassel. For a luxurious effect, use a double-sided ribbon. Narrow satins and taffetas are good choices. The hanging loop can be made from the same ribbon or a decorative cording.

①

②

③

④

⑤

⑥

① Determine the desired finished length of the tassel. Multiply that measurement by 2 and add 1" (2.5 cm) to 1½" (3.8 cm). Cut a piece of cardboard to that dimension. A 3" (7.6 cm) tassel can be wound on a piece of cardboard that is 7" (17.8 cm) to 7½" (19.1 cm) wide.

② Cut a length of ribbon for the hanger and knot the ends together with a double overhand knot. This knot will be hidden inside the head of the tassel. Cut two 5" (12.7 cm) lengths of floral wire and set aside.

③ Wrap the ribbon around the cardboard for half the desired fullness of the finished tassel.

④ Slide the ribbon off the cardboard and hold the middle of the loops securely in one hand. Hold the ribbon loops vertically and cut the top loops. Carefully place the knot of the hanger into the center of the top ribbons, holding it with your fingers at the center of the loops. Wire the ribbons together, just above the knot, making sure that the hanger loop is centered.

⑤ Bring the ribbons coming from the top down and around the hanger knot. Arrange ribbons around the hanger and hold them tight just below the inside hanger knot. Wrap the neck of the tassel with wire.

⑥ Cut the bottom loops and trim all the ribbon ends. Glue or sew a length of ribbon around the neck of the tassel to cover the wire.

QUICK AND EASY RIBBON TASSEL

A Trim-Tool fringe and tassel maker is like having a third hand and can make simple ribbon tassels in different sizes. Following the manufacturers instructions, decide how long you want the tassel to be, set the guide and wrap the ribbon around the tassel maker as many times as needed for the thickness of tassel you want to make. The sample shown is 4" (10.2 cm) and was made with eighteen wraps of ribbon for a total of thirty-six cut ends at the bottom.

Tightly tie off the top loop with narrow ribbon. Wrap narrow ribbon around the neck of the ribbon twice and tie tightly.

Cut ribbon loops at the bottom and remove tassel from tool.

Thread ends of neck tying ribbon through a large-eyed needle and bury them into the tassel; trim excess. Trim all ribbon ends evenly.

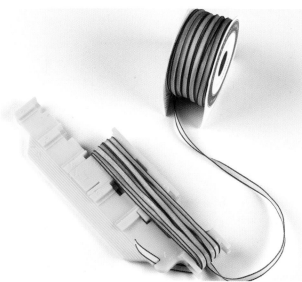

LOOPY RIBBON TASSEL

Like the basic tassel, the loopy ribbon tassel is formed on a piece of cardboard. The loops are not cut and are tied together at one end with the hanger ribbon. A felt bead is added underneath the knot to give the head of the tassel a round shape. The neck and the top of the head can be decorated with small premade ribbon flowers. The loopy tassel looks lush when made with hand-dyed silk ribbons, along with coordinating sheers and satins. For a more casual loopy ribbon tassel, grosgrain and taffeta ribbons, along with rick-rack and other coordinating yarns or trims, can be wound together on the cardboard.

The loopy tassel shown is made on a piece of cardboard that is 7½" (19.1 cm) wide.

YOU WILL NEED

- six different ribbons, 2 yd (1.8 m) long

- ½ yd (0.5 m) additional of one ribbon is needed for the hanger (For a different size tassel, use a wider or narrower cardboard and more or less ribbon.)

- 1" (2.5 cm) felt bead

- needle and thread

- twelve small premade ribbon flowers

- glue (optional)

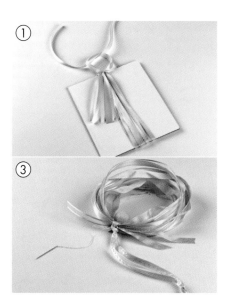

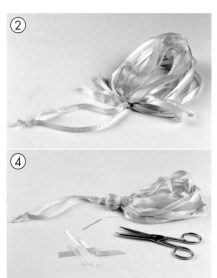

① Holding all ribbons together, wind them around the cardboard. Begin winding with the ribbon ends at the middle of one side of the cardboard. End with the remaining ribbon ends at the middle of the opposite side of the cardboard. Slip the hanger loop under all the ribbons at one end of the cardboard and tightly tie the ends together with a square knot. This will form the top of the tassel's head.

② Carefully remove the loops from the cardboard. Tie the hanger ribbon into an overhand knot close to the top of the head of the tassel. Tie the ends of the hanger ribbon into an overhand knot and trim.

③ Stitch the felt bead to the inside top of the tassel.

④ Hold the ribbons around the bottom of the bead, and stitch or wrap with thread to form the neck of the tassel.

Make sure that the felt bead is completely covered on all sides with ribbon.

⑤ Trim cut ends of ribbon next to the neck. Glue or stitch ribbon flowers around the neck of the tassel and at the top of the head.

RIBBON TASSEL WITH PAINTED WOOD HEAD

This loopy ribbon tassel features a head made from unpainted wood components—a candle cup, toy wheel, and dowel cap. The pieces are glued together and painted in colors to coordinating with the ribbon. The skirt is formed by first creating a ribbon fringe and rolling it to fit inside the head. Since the skirt requires a fair amount of yardage, knitting ribbons are good to use for this project. You can also use a combination of any ribbon remnants in coordinating colors.

YOU WILL NEED

- ¾ yd (0.7 m) ⅜" (9 mm) satin ribbon for tassel skirt
- eighteen ⅓-yd (30 cm) lengths of ⅜" (9 mm) knitting ribbon
- ½ yd (0.5 m) ¼" (7 mm) ribbon for hanger loop
- 1⅝" (4.1 cm) unpainted wood candle cup
- 1½" (3.8 cm) unpainted wood toy wheel
- ½" (1.3 cm) unpainted wood dowel cap
- drill with small bit
- wood glue
- acrylic paint in colors to match ribbons
- fine sand paper
- clear acrylic gloss sealer
- paint brush
- sewing machine and thread
- hot glue and glue gun
- 9" (23 cm) floral wire

① Drill a hole into the center of the dowel cap. To create the tassel head, glue the wheel to the candle cup and the dowel cap to the wheel. To allow for the hanger loop to be attached, make sure the holes align. Allow glue to dry.

② Paint tassel head with a base coat of paint. Add two or three more coats of paint. Let paint dry between coats, and lightly sand between layers. Use contrasting colors to paint various sections of the head. If desired, lines, dots, and squiggles can be added. When completely dry, apply sealer following manufacturer's instructions.

③ To make the skirt, cut knitting ribbon into sixty-six 10" (25.4 cm) lengths. These lengths will be sewn to the ⅜" (9 mm) satin ribbon. At one end of the satin ribbon, lower a machine needle into center of ribbon. Fold a knitting ribbon length in half, and align raw edges with outer edge of satin ribbon. Machine-stitch ribbon loop to satin ribbon. Fold another length of knitting ribbon in half and sew it next to the first loop. Continue to stitch all ribbon loops to the satin ribbon, creating a loopy fringe.

④ Starting at one end, roll fringe, aligning satin ribbon edges, and glue.

Wrap the entire fringe into a tight roll that will fit into the bottom opening of the tassel head. Test to make sure it fits snugly into place. You can add or remove ribbon loops if needed to obtain a good fit.

⑤ To attach the hanger, fold ¼" (7 mm) ribbon in half, and knot the ends. Fold the wire in half to make a "needle" for threading the hanger. Loop the wire through the hanger loop and draw it through the holes in the head. A drop of glue can be added to the knot to keep it secure to the inside of the head.

⑥ Glue rolled tassel skirt into the opening at the bottom of the tassel head.

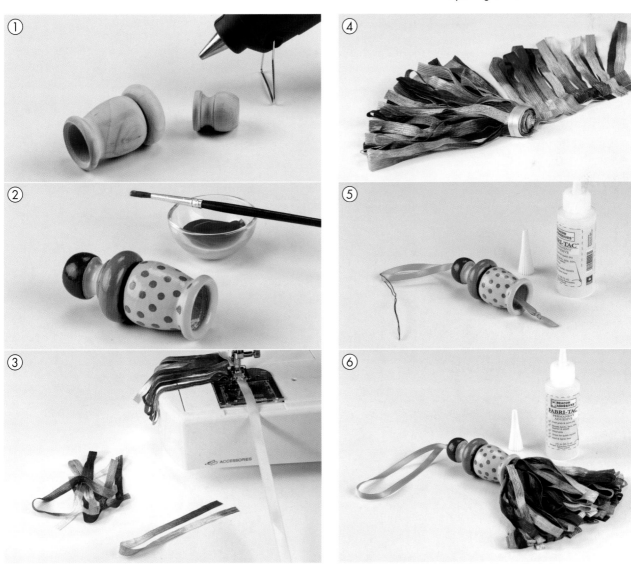

RIBBON WEAVING,
PATCHWORK,
AND KNITTING

Experimenting with ribbons and traditional textile techniques, such as weaving, patchwork, and knitting, can lead to exciting projects. Ribbons can be combined with yarns, fabrics, and threads, or used exclusively, to make home décor or personal items that have interesting textures and color combinations.

Woven Ribbon Fabrics

Ribbons in an array of colors, sizes, and patterns create exquisite fabrics when woven together and fused onto an iron-on backing. Woven ribbon fabrics can be used to construct a pillow, placemat, or picture frame. They can be incorporated into parts of a garment or made into gift items such as handbags, sachets, book covers, or glasses cases.

A padded pinning board, marked with a grid, is extremely handy for weaving ribbons. A well-padded ironing board can be used, if it is large enough to accommodate the desired finished size of the woven ribbon fabric. Ribbons can also be woven on a cork board, provided that layers of padding are added and the board can withstand the heat of an iron.

In addition, you will need lightweight iron-on interfacing, glass-headed pins, an iron and pressing cloth, and a bodkin, elastic guide or large-eyed blunt needle.

There are three steps involved in making woven ribbon fabric—preparing the interfacing, weaving the ribbons, and fusing the ribbons.

PREPARING THE INTERFACING

Determine the size ribbon fabric you want to weave and cut a square or rectangle of iron-on interfacing to fit that dimension plus 1" (2.5 cm) seam allowance on all sides. With the adhesive side up, pin the interfacing at the corners to the padded surface.

WEAVING THE RIBBONS

As with other woven fabrics, the vertical ribbons will be referred to as the warp, and the horizontal ribbons will be the weft.

Cut ribbon lengths for the warp rows 2" (5 cm) longer than the vertical dimension of the interfacing. Place the ribbons side by side over the interfacing. The ribbon edges should not overlap; depending upon the thickness of the ribbon and the selected weave, a very slight space can be left between the warp ribbons. Pin each ribbon at the top and bottom, angling the pins away from the center of the weaving. Make sure that the right sides of the ribbons are facing up. The wrong side of the ribbons will be fused to the interfacing.

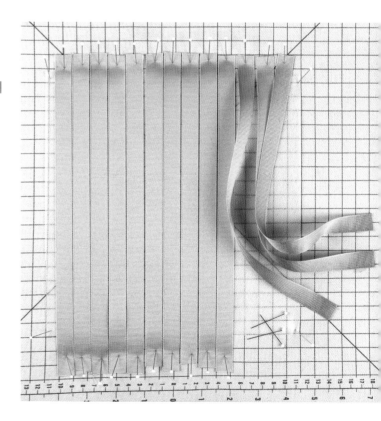

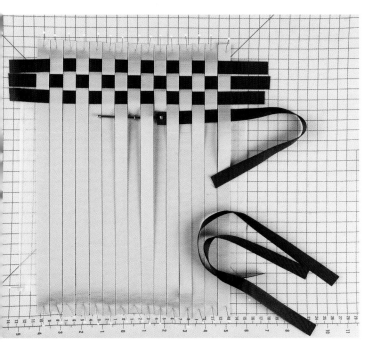

Cut ribbon lengths for the weft rows 2" (5 cm) longer than the horizontal dimension of the interfacing. Following the instructions for the desired weave pattern, use a bodkin, elastic guide, or large-eyed needle to weave the weft ribbons through the warp ribbons. Begin the weaving at the top row and work down, pulling every row taut and straight, and abutting edges as closely as possible. Repin and adjust warp rows as necessary. Pin each weft ribbon at the sides of the weaving. If your last weft row extends beyond the bottom edge of the weaving area, push the weft ribbons closer together or eliminate the last weft ribbon.

FUSING THE RIBBONS

Make sure all ribbon rows are straight and smooth. Cover the woven ribbon fabric with a press cloth. With a dry iron on a moderate setting, light press to partially fuse the interfacing to the back of the all the ribbon rows. Make sure to press the ribbons at the outer edges with the tip of the iron. Remove pins and place weaving face down on the ironing surface. With a moderately hot steam setting (or a damp press cloth and moderately hot iron), press the ribbons securely to the interfacing. Allow the weaving to cool before handling.

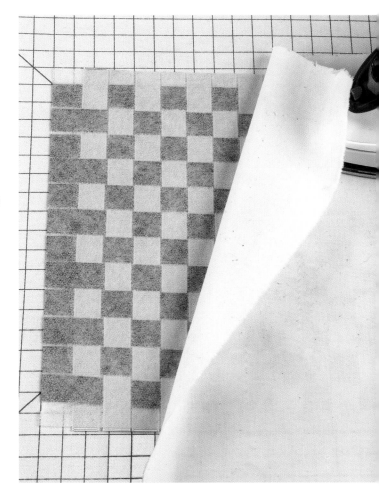

MAKING A SAMPLE AND ESTIMATING RIBBON LENGTH

It is a good idea to make a test sample of the selected weave pattern, using different ribbon colors and size arrangements to determine the most desirable look for your weaving project. This chart gives the approximate quantities of ribbons needed to weave a fabric using the same width of ribbon throughout the weaving. If you are using two colors of ribbon, for example one for the warp and one for the weft, you would need to divide the total yardage stated by 2 to get the length needed for each color of ribbon. Lengths are given for two-way weaves, such as plain, basket, and twill, as well as the three-way tumbling block pattern.

RIBBON WIDTH	TOTAL LENGTH NEEDED		
Two-way weaves	4" (10 cm) square	8" (20.5 cm) square	12" (20.5 cm) square
³⁄₁₆" (5 mm)	6½ yd (5.9 m)	22 yd (20.3 m)	46 yd (42.5 m)
¼" (7 mm)	4½ yd (4.1 m)	16 yd (14.7 m)	33 yd (30.4 m)
³⁄₈" (9 mm)	3¾ yd (3.45 m)	12 yd (11 m)	25 yd (23 m)
½" (12 mm)	3¼ yd (3 m)	9¾ yd (8.5 m)	20¼ yd (18.7 m)
⅝" (15 mm)	2½ yd (2.3 m)	7¼ yd (6.6 m)	15¼ yd (14 m)
⅞" (23 mm)	1½ yd (1.4 m)	5 yd (4.6 m)	10 yd (9.1 m)
RIBBON WIDTH	LENGTH FOR EACH RIBBON		
Tumbling Blocks	4" (10 cm) square	8" (20.5 cm) square	12" (30.5 cm) square
³⁄₁₆" (5 mm)	3½ yd (3.2 m)	12 yd (11 m)	25 yd (23 m)
¼" (7 mm)	2½ yd (2.3 m)	9 yd (8.3 m)	18½ yd (17 m)
³⁄₈" (9 mm)	2¼ yd (2.1 m)	7 yd (6.4 m)	14½ yd (13.4 m)
½" (12 mm)	2 yd (1.8 m)	5½ yd (5 m)	12 yd (11 m)
⅝" (15 mm)	1½ yd (1.4 m)	4¼ yd (3.9 m)	10 yd (9.1 m)
⅞" (23 mm)	1 yd (0.9 m)	3½ yd (3.2 m)	7 yd (6.4 m)

RIBBON WEAVE PATTERNS

Weaving the ribbons over and under each other in different repetitive rows can create a variety of patterns. By experimenting with the placement of the warp and weft ribbon colors within these patterns, you will discover additional effects.

Plain weave

Pass the weft ribbon over one warp ribbon, under one, over one, under one, continuing across the row. Reverse the pattern for each succeeding row.

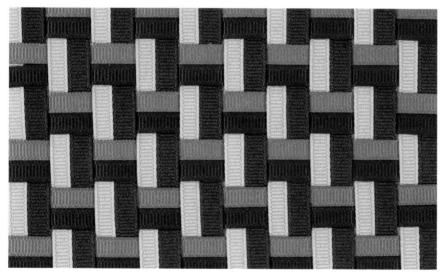

Basket weave

Pass the weft ribbon over two warps, under two, over two, under two, continuing across the row. Repeat this pattern for the next row. Reverse the pattern for the next two rows. Continue alternating the two rows weaving pattern.

WOVEN RIBBON TRIM

Like ribbon fabric, this trim is woven and fused onto lightweight iron-on interfacing. Only three warp ribbons are needed. Measure the width of the three ribbons and cut the interfacing by that width and the desired finished length of the trim. The weft ribbon is woven in a plain weave. At each side of the trim, the weft ribbon is folded, overlapped, and inserted into the next row of weaving. Select a double-faced ribbon for the weft, as both sides will show when the points are formed. Use pins to hold the folded points in place while weaving; iron weaving to interfacing and press weft points at each side. A pattern ribbon, or lace, used in the warp adds a feminine touch. A sportier trim can be made by using grosgrain and stripe ribbons.

Twill

Pass the weft ribbon over two warps, under one, over two, under one, continuing across. In the second row and each succeeding row, shift the pattern one warp ribbon to the right, creating a diagonal pattern.

If alternating light and dark ribbon colors are used in both the warp and weft, a diagonal zigzag is created.

Patchwork weave

A patchwork of ribbons can be woven by using three colors of ribbon for the warp and weft, and alternating the number of warps the weft passes over and under with each row. Patterned ribbons add to the patchwork effect.

The warp ribbons for the sample shown are placed in the following order from left to right: ribbon A (green), ribbon B (stripe), ribbon A (green), ribbon C (blue dot).

Starting at the top right of the weaving: weave row 1—weft color A over warp A & B, under warp A & C, repeat across. Weave row 2—weft color B under warp A, over warp B, under warp A, over warp C, repeat across. Weave row 3—weft color A under A, over B & A, under C & A, over B & A, repeat across. Weave row 4—weft color C over A, under B, over A & C & A, under B, over A & C & A, repeat across. Repeat these four rows to create the patchwork weave.

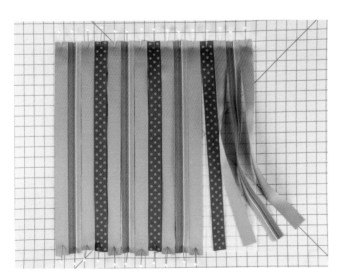

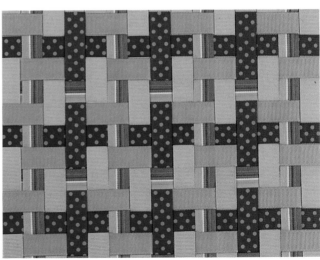

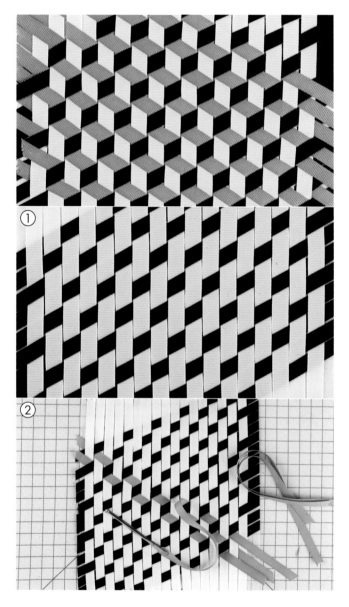

Tumbling blocks

By careful selection of ribbon colors, this three-way ribbon weave creates the optical illusion of the tumbling block quilting pattern. As with other weaves, the warp ribbons run vertically. Instead of one horizontal direction for the weft ribbons, two sets of diagonal wefts are woven through the warp.

① Select three contrasting ribbons for this pattern—one color for the warp, a second color for the first set of diagonal wefts, and a third color for the second set of diagonal wefts. Each of the ribbons should be the same width. Pin the warp ribbons in place. The first set of diagonal wefts is woven from the upper right of the weaving to lower left. Instead of weaving straight across in a horizontal direction, angle the ribbon down 30 degrees. Weave the first row under 2 warps, over 1 warp, under 2, over 1, to the end. Shift the pattern by 1 ribbon with each row.

② The second set of weft ribbons is woven from lower right to upper left at a 30 degree angle above horizontal. Weave over two warps, under one warp, and the two adjacent wefts from the first set, repeat. Shift the pattern 1 ribbon with each row.

The flap for this handbag was cut from a piece of ribbon weaving created with a color variation of the tumbling block pattern. The warp consists of two colors of ribbon: one warp of black, two warps of gold, repeating across the weaving. Both diagonal weft rows also alternate one black ribbon with two gold ribbons through the weaving. When the gold ribbons cross, a star pattern appears.

WOVEN RIBBON BRACELET

Besides weaving ribbons together to make a fabric, ribbons can be woven onto a base, such as a foam wreath form, or directly onto a project, such as a purchased pillow. This ribbon bracelet was woven on an unfinished wood bracelet.

Variation

A narrower bracelet can be wrapped with ⅛" (3 mm) ribbon. By adding a few wraps between the pattern rows, a cross shape can be woven.

YOU WILL NEED

- 1" (2.5 cm) wide unfinished flat wood bracelet
- 3 yd (2.7 m) of ¼" (7 mm) grosgrain ribbon for wrapping*
- 1 yd (0.9 m) contrasting ¼" (7 mm) grosgrain ribbon for the wraps*
- tacky glue
- large-eyed needle

①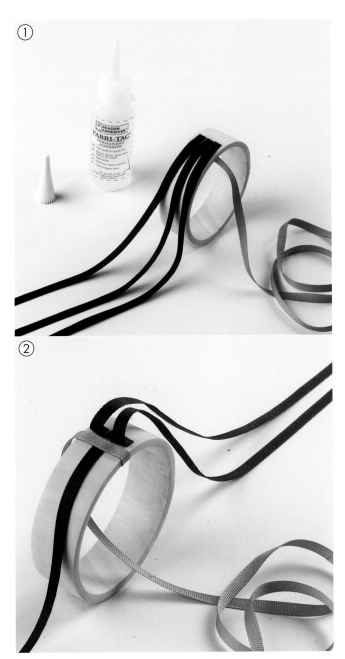

②

③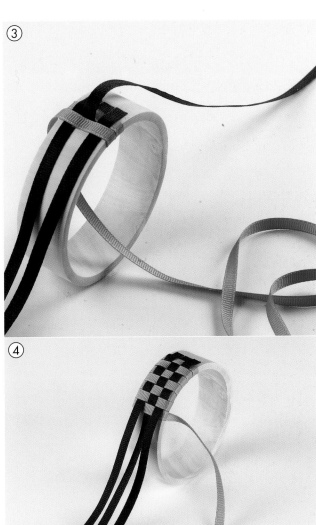

④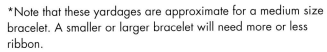

*Note that these yardages are approximate for a medium size bracelet. A smaller or larger bracelet will need more or less ribbon.

① Cut 1 yd (0.9 m) ribbon into three 12" (30.5 cm) lengths. Glue one end of each ribbon to the front of the bracelet. These warp ribbons should lie side by side, and the ribbons should only be glued to the bracelet at one end. Glue one end of the remaining ribbon to the inside of the bracelet. Allow the glue to dry.

② Begin to wrap the ribbon around to the front of the bracelet. Fold back the two outer warps and continue wrapping for one pass. The winding ribbon will cover the center warp.

③ For the second wrap, fold back the center warp and continue wrapping. The winding ribbon will cover the two outer warps, creating a checkerboard appearance.

④ Repeat pattern as the entire bracelet is wrapped. At the end, thread the individual warp ribbons into a large-eyed needle and tuck them under the winding ribbon. Cut excess winding ribbon and glue the end to the inside of the bracelet.

Weaving ribbons through

In addition to weaving ribbons together or onto a base, ribbons can be woven through a variety of materials.

A length of ribbon woven through eyelet beading adds an elegant accent to a plain guest towel. Cut the lace about 1" (2.5 cm) wider than the width of the towel. Thread ribbon through the lace and machine- or hand-stitch the lace to the edge of the towel, turning back and stitching the raw edges at each side.

Laces designed with slits or holes to accommodate narrow ribbons are known as beading trims. You will find them as an insertion trim (straight edges on both sides) or an edging trim (one edge is unfinished and is meant to be attached to the edge of your project). Use a bodkin, elastic guide, or large-eyed needle to thread the ribbon through the trim. Select a ribbon width that will fit the slits in the lace, fill the holes, and lie smoothly.

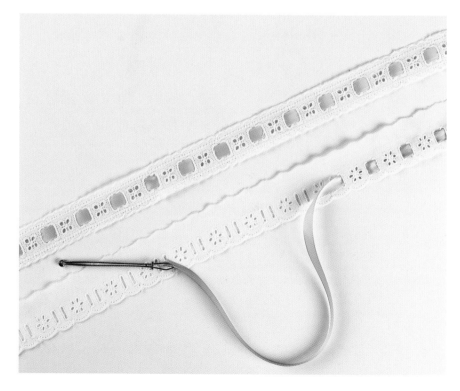

Gluing the ribbon-woven trim to a placemat or purchased pillow is a quick and easy way to make a unique accent for your home or to give as a gift.

Search the home décor department in the fabric store and look for trims that have openings large enough for weaving a length of ribbon. This heavy trim is perfect for adding a row of ⅜" (9 mm) grosgrain ribbon.

To weave the ribbon, use a bodkin or needle that will fit into the spaces between the hem stitches. Two and a half yards of ⅞" (23 mm) sheer ribbon was used to weave through the hemstitches of this 20" (50.8 cm) napkin. Begin by centering the ribbon at one corner and weaving out in both directions. The trick is to not pull the ribbon too tightly through the spaces. Leave it a little loose on the front and allow the ribbon to "pouf." Experiment with the number of spaces to skip between each pouf. Adjust the spacing along each edge of the linen so that the pattern will be even at the corners of the project. Overlap and slipstitch the raw edges of the ribbon together where they meet on the back. Wash ribbon-woven linens on gentle in cold water and lay flat to dry. Iron while still damp; be careful to not let the hot iron scorch the ribbon.

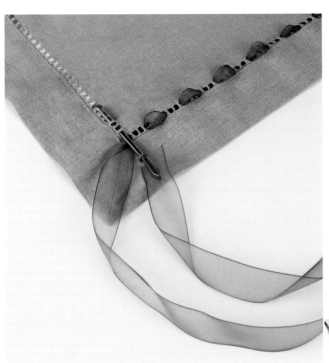

Weaving soft, sheer ribbon through plain hem-stitched linen napkins, placemats, and tablecloths dresses up your dining table for entertaining.

 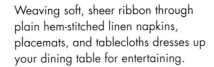

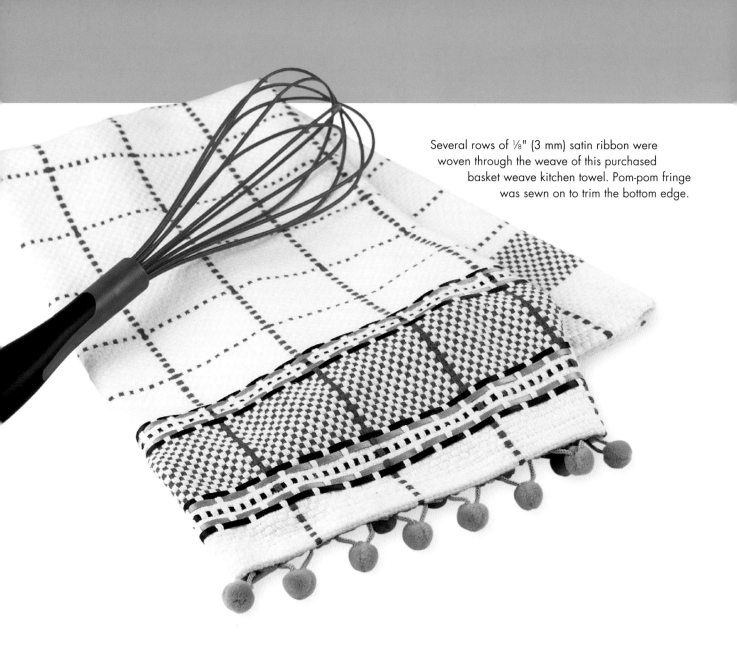

Several rows of ⅛" (3 mm) satin ribbon were woven through the weave of this purchased basket weave kitchen towel. Pom-pom fringe was sewn on to trim the bottom edge.

Monk's cloth is a soft cotton basket-weave fabric used for making afghans, pillows, towels, placemats, and table runners. Narrow ribbons threaded through a blunt large-eyed needle can be evenly woven through the basket weave structure of monk's cloth. By skipping spaces and varying the length of the stitches, simple patterns can be achieved. This type of weaving, known as huck embroidery or Swedish weaving, is traditionally stitched with yarn but ⅛" (3 mm) ribbon can be used for a different look.

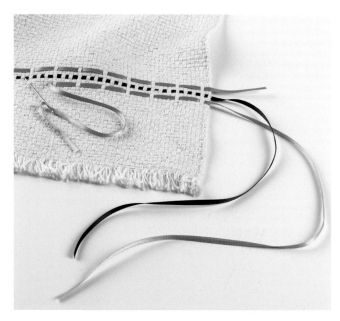

Look for plastic trays and totes or wicker baskets with holes that can accommodate a few rows of ribbon weaving. Three rows of ribbon were woven into this inexpensive tray to make a small catch-all to keep scissors, threads, pins, etc., close at hand while sewing. The ribbons overlapped at the front and are glued to the basket. A bow with button center covers the join.

Narrow ribbons can be used for cross stitch and Swedish weaving or huck embroidery designs. They also can be drawn through hand-smocking stitches or the pulled threads of coarsely woven fabrics. Narrow ribbons can also be embroidered on mesh or canvas to create a needlepoint effect.

It's fun to experiment and see what other textile techniques can include ribbon. A touch of ribbon can add dimension to needle felting projects. Loops of ribbons were placed underneath precut felt flowers before they were needle felted to this felt bag. Silk embroidery ribbon was used to tie on the button flower centers and ribbon stitches were added to each large petal.

Ribbon Patchwork

Woven-edge ribbons, placed side-by-side, can imitate the look of traditional patchwork patterns, such as log cabin. Because they have no raw edges, the ribbons may be fused to interfacing, as done with ribbon weaving, or can be glued or sewn to a base fabric, or placed directly onto the project material. The cut edges of the ribbons will be covered by the overlapping rows of the patchwork pattern. The abutted edges may be left unfinished or be further embellished with hand or machine stitching. A crazy patchwork is created by selecting a range of ribbon colors, types, and patterns.

LOG CABIN

This patchwork block starts with a center square of ribbon. Surrounding rows are positioned around the square.

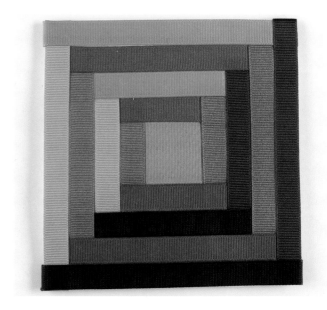

In this sample, a 2" (5 cm) square of 1½" (39 mm) pink ribbon is placed in the center. A length of ⅝" (15 mm) red ribbon is placed on the bottom and along one side. A length of brown ⅝" (15 mm) ribbon is placed at the top and along the remaining side of the square. Make sure that the ribbons overlap so that the center ribbon is 1½" (39 mm) square. In the same way, ⅝" (15 mm) orange and dark brown ribbons are added around the square for the next row. Alternating the colors of the rows adds to the pattern.

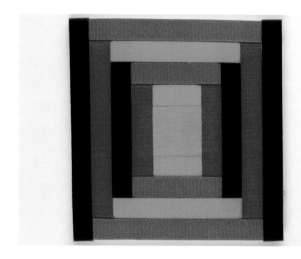

COURTHOUSE STEPS

A variation of the log cabin pattern, courthouse steps also starts with a center square of ribbon. Surrounding rows are placed in horizontal and vertical positions around the square.

In this sample, a 2" (5 cm) square of 1½" (39 mm) orange ribbon is placed in the center. A length of ⅝" (15 mm) pink ribbon is placed at the top and bottom, making sure that the center square is 1½" (39 mm). A length of ⅝" (15 mm) red ribbon is placed at each side. For the next rows, a length of ⅝" (15 mm) brown ribbon is added to the top and bottom, and ⅝" (15 mm) dark brown ribbon is added to the sides. The colors alternate for the additional rows.

RIBBON PATCHWORK PILLOWS

The design of these beautiful jacquard ribbons inspired the color combinations for two ribbon patchwork pillows. The jacquard ribbons were cut to showcase the motifs at the center of the patchwork blocks. The ribbons were fused to a square of wool felt cut to the size of the finished pillow plus seam allowances. The outside ribbon rows of the blocks were extended to the edges of the felt and were caught into the seams when the back felt square was sewn to the front. Machine zigzag stitches were sewn at the edges where the ribbons abut. The aqua and brown pillow was constructed in a log cabin pattern. The orange and fuchsia pillow was made following the courthouse steps pattern.

Knitting with Ribbon

Soft narrow ribbons, as well as ribbons designed specifically for knitting, can be knit in the same way as regular yarns. Simple garter and stockinette patterns look best when knitting with ribbon. Make sure to use smooth needles with blunt points so as not to snag or pierce the ribbon when knitting. The ribbon will want to twist up on itself and trying to keep it perfectly flat is nearly impossible. The twists add to the texture of the knitted fabric. However, the ribbons should not be so tightly twisted that they pull up on themselves. Stop every few rows and dangle the yarn to allow the twist to work itself down the ribbon. Or, place the ball of ribbon into a small mesh bag or knee-high stocking to keep it neat as you knit.

THE COMPLETE PHOTO GUIDE TO RIBBON CRAFTS

RIBBON WOVEN KNIT SCARF

Ribbons can be combined with regular yarns in interesting ways. This ribbon woven slip-stitch scarf is made by first knitting the base of the scarf and then weaving the ribbons through the spaces left by the dropped stitches.

YOU WILL NEED

- 1 skein lightweight worsted or DK cotton or cotton-blend yarn (a smooth yarn makes it easier to weave the ribbons through the spaces of the dropped stitches)

- narrow satin, knitting, or silk ribbons in colors to coordinate with yarn; the scarf shown used 20 yd (18 m) of ⅛" (3 mm) and 10 yd (9 m) of ⅜" (9 mm) satin ribbon

- knitting needles, #8 and #10

- large blunt yarn/tapestry needle

① Cast on 12 stitches with a #10 needle.

② Row 1: Change to #8 needles. Knit 2, yarn over; repeat 5 times. End row with knit 2. A total of 17 stitches will now be on the needle.

③ Row 2 and all following rows: Knit every row. Knit until you have used almost all of the yarn.

④ Change to #10 needles and loosely bind off as follows: knit 2, pass the first stitch over the second, drop the third stitch off the needle. *Knit 1, pass the first stitch over the second on the needle, drop the next stitch off the needle. Repeat from * to the end of the row. You will have dropped 5 stitches.

⑤ Holding the sides of the scarf and with gentle pressure, pull the scarf to cause the dropped stitches to "run" down the entire length, creating 5 rows for weaving the ribbons.

⑥ Cut the ribbons into lengths the measurement of the finished scarf plus 18" (45.7 cm). Thread each ribbon onto the needle and weave the ribbons in and out of the bars formed by the dropped stitches. Weave three ribbons into each row.

⑦ Form an overhand knot to secure each group of ribbons at the ends of the scarf. Trim ribbon fringe to an even length.

⑥

SEW AND NO-SEW
RIBBON TECHNIQUES

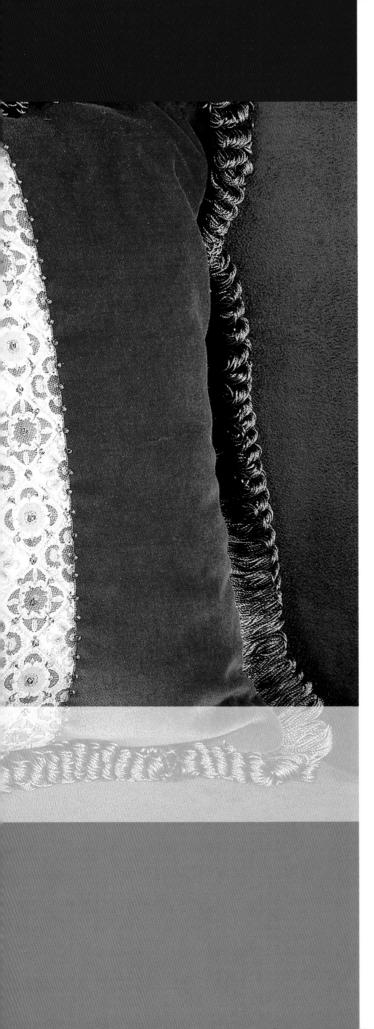

Ribbons can be attached to projects in many ways. Machine- or hand-stitching is traditional, and is the best method if the finished project will be washed frequently or will get a lot of wear and tear. However for many projects, with the vast array of adhesive products on the market, ribbons can be easily glued, taped, and fused so no sewing is required.

Sewing with Ribbons

When trimming wearable or home décor projects with ribbon, sewing is often the best method. If the finished item is to be washed, make sure to preshrink the base fabric by washing and drying it before applying the ribbons. Although most ribbons on the market today are shrink resistant and color fast, you may want to wash and dry the ribbons too.

TIPS FOR SEWING RIBBONS

- When machine stitching, always sew in the same direction on both sides of the ribbon. This will prevent puckering.

- Use a sharp needle to assure that the ribbon will not snag when stitched. The needle should be fine enough so the holes it creates in the ribbon are just large enough for the sewing thread.

- Make a sample to test stitch length and machine tension. Use straight stitches, narrow zigzag, or overcast stitches that will just catch the edge of the ribbon.

- Use polyester thread; machine embroidery thread may also work for more densely sewn machine decorative stitches. Coordinate the thread color with the ribbon. Match the ribbon color for a less visible attachment or select a contrasting color for added interest.

- Plan the design and calculate the total amount of ribbon needed, allowing for seams and neatening the ends.

- Iron ribbons to remove any creases. Be careful when ironing printed ribbons as the designs may smear when heated. Test the ribbon and adjust the iron temperature, use a press cloth, and press with an up and down motion rather than sliding the iron across the ribbon.

- Stitching the ribbons to the flat fabric before the project is constructed will allow for the raw edges of the ribbons to be caught in the seam allowance. If trimming a ready-made article, open up the seams a little to allow the ribbon joins to be hidden inside. Or, turn the cut edges under for a neat finish at each end.

- Use dressmaker's chalk or air-soluble marker and ruler to mark positions of ribbons.

- Strips of fusible web or a fabric glue stick can help to keep ribbons in place while stitching. Test and make sure that the adhered ribbon can be easily stitched without the adhesive gumming up the needle. Some adhesives are not made to be stitched through.

- If you prefer to sew the ribbons by hand, use a tiny hem stitch to catch just the edge of the ribbon to the project. Or, use embroidery floss and decorative stitches to add more detail.

HAND SEWING RIBBONS

Hand stitching is best to use for sewing velvet and intricate jacquard ribbons to a project. While machine stitching may show or interfere with the design of the ribbon, hand slipstitches close to the edge of the ribbon provide an almost invisible finish. Use a fine needle and select a thread color that matches the edge of the ribbon.

This beautiful jacquard ribbon was hand-sewn to the velveteen background fabric before the pillow was constructed. For added detail, small seed beads were added as each slipstitch was sewn. Additional beads were sewn to highlight areas of the ribbon design.

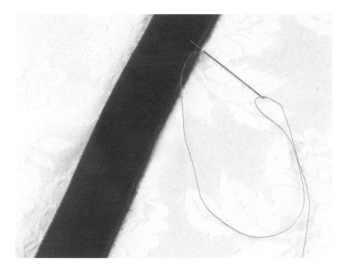

To form slipstitches, bring a threaded needle to the front of the background fabric. Take a tiny stitch just into the edge of the ribbon. Bring the thread back into the fabric, making stitches every ¼" (6 mm) and spacing them evenly along the length of the ribbon.

MACHINE SEWING RIBBONS

Create a custom boutique look for your bathroom by simply machine-stitching a length of ribbon onto the ends of plain towels. If desired, a washable trim can be stitched to the bottom of the towel.

A few rows of ribbon can be stitched to the edge of a napkin or tablecloth to make an interlacing woven pattern. Sew one row of ribbon parallel to one edge of the project. Sew another ribbon along another edge, overlapping the previous ribbon at the corner. Continue to position and sew rows of ribbon equal distance from the previous rows.

FOLDED AND STITCHED RIBBON DESIGNS

Popular during Victorian times, folded and stitched ribbon patterns can be used to elegantly decorate towels, sheets, and curtains.

Make sure to select a ribbon that is double-sided, or has an interesting reverse side, as both sides of the ribbon will show when it is folded into the design. A ribbon that is not slippery, such as a grosgrain or jacquard, will be easier to work with and will keep its shape when the ribbon is manipulated into folds. The pattern can be planned and drawn onto paper, and then transferred to the fabric. Or, the designs can be pinned and formed directly on the project. Measure carefully to create a balanced and centered design. Stitch the ribbons close to the edges.

DECORATIVE MACHINE STITCHING

Most sewing machines have built-in embroidery stitches that are fun to use for attaching ribbons. Experiment with the width and length of the stitches and different types and colors of thread. You may need to adjust the thread and/or bobbin tension of your machine. If the stitches cause puckering, add one or two layers of stabilizer under the fabric.

MITERED RIBBON CORNERS

Mitering is a neat way to attach ribbons around right-angle corners of a project, such as a tablecloth, placemat, or napkin. The ribbon is folded back on itself to create diagonal lines at the corners. This stitching technique is particularly attractive when a wide striped ribbon is used.

① Position the ribbon parallel to one side of the project. Stitch close to the outer edge. End the stitches at the point where the corner should be.

② Fold the ribbon back on itself and then diagonally to the side. Press to mark the stitching line between the inner and outer edges of the ribbon.

③ Open diagonal fold. Beginning at the outer corner of the ribbon, stitch on the diagonal crease through the ribbon and the project. End the stitching at the inner corner of the ribbon.

④ Trim seam if ribbon is bulky or shows when the corner is turned. Press. Continue to edge stitch ribbon around project, mitering remaining corners. Edge stitch inner edge in one continuous seam.

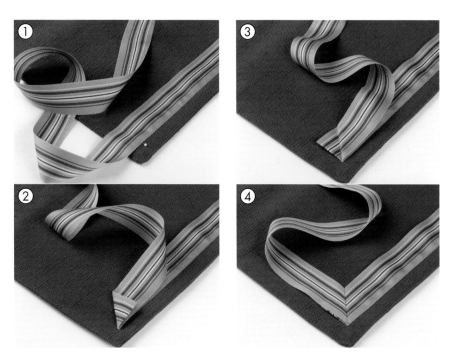

RIBBON CASINGS

A ribbon makes an attractive casing for a drawstring or elastic.
Select a ribbon a little wider than the drawstring or elastic. Sew it
to the project close to both edges, turning back the raw edges at
the ends. Use a bodkin, large needle, or elastic guide to insert the
drawstring or elastic.

Ribbon drawstring bag

Sew an easy ribbon-trimmed drawstring pouch for a special
gift bag.

① Cut a rectangle of fabric the desired width of the pouch
plus ½" (1.3 cm) by 2 times the desired length plus 1"
(2.5 cm). Fold fabric in half, right sides together, and stitch ¼"
(6 mm) side seams. Turn pouch right side out. Fold and stitch a
double ¼" (6 mm) hem at the top of the bag.

② To make the casing, cut two lengths of ⅞" (2.2 cm) ribbon
the width of the pouch plus 1" (2.5 cm). Stitch them equal
distance from the top, turning back the raw edges so that the
ribbons end at the side seams.

③ Cut two lengths of ⅜" (9 mm) ribbon for the drawstring.
Insert one ribbon at one side of the casing and thread it
around the pouch. Knot the ends together. Insert the remaining
ribbon at the opposite casing and knot the ends.

If desired, lengths of ribbon can be stitched to the fabric
before the side seams are sewn.

②

③

RIBBON LOOP FRINGE

Short lengths of ribbons, folded and sewn around a project, create a fun loop fringe. Stitch the ribbons to the sides of throws or pillows and also to ready-made garments, such as the hem of a little girl's jeans.

YOU WILL NEED

- 30" × 40" (76.2 × 101.6 cm) rectangle of flannel

- 30" × 40" (76.2 × 101.6 cm) rectangle of flannel-backed satin for lining

- 4 yd (3.6 m) of ⅞" (23 mm) satin ribbon

- 4" (10.2 cm) lengths of coordinating ribbons for fringe; select a variety of ribbon types and widths. The sample shown uses approximately 200 loops.

- sewing machine and thread

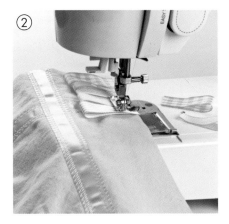
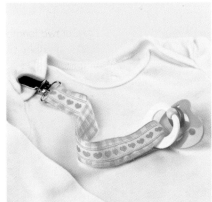
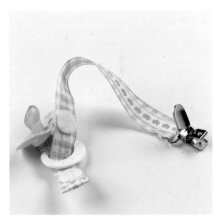

RIBBON FRINGE BABY BLANKET

① Use straight or decorative stitches to attach ⅞" (23 mm) ribbon 2½" (6.4 cm) from all sides of the flannel rectangle.

② Starting ½" (1.3 cm) from one corner of the flannel rectangle, fold a ribbon length in half, and align raw edges with edge of flannel. Stitch ¼" (6 mm) from edge. Continue to fold and stitch ribbon loops side by side along one side, ending ½" (1.3 cm) from the corner. Add ribbon loops to all four sides.

③ Right sides together, stitch satin lining to flannel, following fringe stitching line, and leaving an opening for turning. Turn right sides out and slipstitch opening closed.

Make a coordinating pacifier clip by stitching a 12" (30.5 cm) length of ⅜" (9 mm) ribbon to a 12" (30.5 cm) length of ⅝" (15 mm) ribbon. Thread one end through the loop of a suspender or mitten clip; fold the raw edge under twice and stitch to hold the clip in place. Stitch a double hem at the other end to cover the raw edge. Thread the pacifier onto the ribbon and sew hook-and-loop dots to the ribbon so that the pacifier can be easily removed.

STITCHED RIBBON LACE

Rows of ribbon can be machine-stitched together to form a lacy fabric for a scarf, shawl, or sheer garment. The magic happens when the ribbons are sewn to a water-soluble stabilizer. This type of stabilizer, found in most fabric stores, is used to back and strengthen fabrics when a machine-embroidered design is being stitched. It is strong, translucent, and completely dissolves in cool water.

Straight-stitch rows of ribbon to the stabilizer. Starting at the outside ribbon at one corner, stitch a crosswise row connecting all the ribbons. End with the needle down in the center of the last ribbon. Pivot and turn; stitch up that ribbon for 1" (2.5 cm) or less. End with the needle down. Pivot and turn, and stitch another row back across all the ribbons. Continue to stitch the rows, forming a grid of thread. When the stitching is completed, follow the manufacturer's instructions and submerge the lace in water to remove the stabilizer.

Ribbons can vary from satins to sheers to taffetas, or can all be one type and color. Make sure all ribbons selected for ribbon lace are washable and will not shrink or fade. Use standard sewing or machine embroidery thread for the rows of stitching. It is always a good idea to make a sample to test the ribbons and thread, and to get a feel for stitching onto the stabilizer. Do not be overly concerned about keeping the stitching rows precisely even. Use the machine presser foot as a guide and look through the stabilizer as you sew to see the seam markings on the machine. You may want to experiment with different patterns by angling the ribbon rows and cross stitches.

LACY RIBBON SCARF

The scarf shown is approximately 12" × 72" (30.5 × 183 cm), and uses thirteen rows of ribbon. Make adjustments to the suggested measurements for a smaller or larger scarf.

YOU WILL NEED

- 12" × 60" (30.5 × 152 cm) rectangle of water soluble stabilizer

- twelve to fifteen lengths of various ribbons, each cut 72" (183 cm) long; use ribbons ¼" (7 mm) to ⅞" (23 mm) wide

- sewing machine and thread

① Stitch the center of one ribbon length onto one long edge of the stabilizer. Continue to stitch parallel rows of ribbon filling the width of the stabilizer. It is not necessary to pin the ribbon. Guide it with your hand and use the presser foot to place the stitches in the center of each ribbon.

② Starting at one end, stitch crosswise rows to connect the ribbons. Keep the stitching continuous by pivoting and turning at the outside ribbons. Vary the width of the crosswise rows from ¼" (6 mm) to 1" (2.5 cm).

③ Continue stitching the rows to the center of the scarf. End the stitching at one side ribbon. In the same way, sew crosswise rows from the other end of the scarf toward the center until the entire scarf has been stitched with a grid of thread.

④ Follow manufacturer's instructions to remove the stabilizer in cool water. Rinse well.

⑤ Wrap scarf in towel to remove water. Lay flat to air dry. Trim the ends of each ribbon into a V.

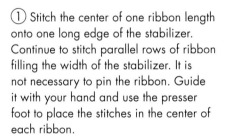

CAKE RIBBON APRON AND DISH TOWEL

Ribbons woven with a design of yummy cakes is the perfect accent for these easy-to-sew kitchen fashions.

YOU WILL NEED

- 1 yd (0.9 m) of 2" (5 cm) ribbon for apron trim
- 2½ yd (2.3 m) of 2¼" (56 cm) grosgrain ribbon for apron waistband and ties
- 36" × 22" (91.4 × 55.9 cm) fabric
- coordinating dish towel
- 1" (25 mm) ribbon to trim the width of the towel plus 1" (2.5 cm)
- fabric strip 3" (7.6 cm) × width of towel plus 1" (2.5 cm)
- pom-pom fringe the width of the towel plus 1" (2.5 cm)
- sewing machine and thread

① To hem apron, press long side of fabric up 2½" (6.4 cm). Press raw edge under ½" (1.3 cm) and stitch. Position 2" (50 mm) ribbon at the stitching line and sew both edges of the ribbon to the fabric. Stitch double ½" (1.3 cm) hems at sides.

② Stitch two rows of long gathering stitches along the top of the apron. Pull threads to gather to 18" (45.7 cm) width. Fold the center 18" (45.7 cm) of waistband ribbon in half and press to crease. Align center of folded ribbon with the center of the top gathered apron. Fold the ribbon to enclose the raw edge of the fabric and pin. Stitch close to the bottom edge of the ribbon waistband, catching in the apron and both sides of the ribbon. Secure the stitches at each side of the apron. The excess ribbon will be used for the apron ties.

③ To trim the towel, sew the 1" (2.5 cm) ribbon to the fabric strip. Turn under ½" (1.3 cm) along all sides of the fabric strip and sew it to the bottom of the towel. Sew the fringe to the edge of the towel.

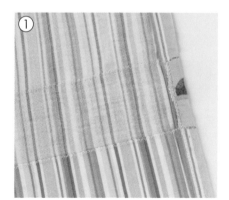

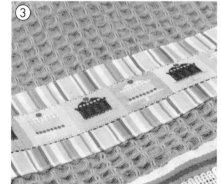

RED & WHITE APRON AND OVEN MITT

Use a purchased dish towel and oven mitt, along with a few ribbons, to make this super quick and cute kitchen set. Not only will the apron keep your clothes clean, you'll always have a towel close at hand to dry your hands.

YOU WILL NEED

- kitchen towel and oven mitt
- two lengths of ⅞" (23 mm) ribbon the width of the towel plus 1" (2.5 cm)
- 2½ yd (2.3 m) of 1½" (39 mm) ribbon for apron waistband and ties
- ½ yd (0.5 m) each of two ⅞" (23 mm) ribbons for oven mitt
- large button
- sewing machine and thread
- needle and thread
- bodkin or large safety pin

① Fold towel so that one side is 2½" (6.4 cm) shorter than the other. Press and stitch close to the fold. To form the casing, stitch 2" (5 cm) from the fold. Thread the 1½" (39 mm) ribbon through the casing and center it so that the ribbon ties are an equal length.

② Stitch ⅞" (23 mm) ribbons to the ends of the towel, turning back the raw edges at the sides.

③ Form two loop bows with the remaining ribbons and sew them together. Stitch the bows to the top of the oven mitt, adding the large button to the center.

Gluing, Fusing, and Taping Ribbons

Different types of adhesives make crafting with ribbons quicker and easier than traditional sewing techniques. Follow the manufacturer's instructions for all adhesive products and test the adhesive with the ribbons you intend to use to make sure that the finished application looks good and the bond is strong. If one product does not work well with the selected materials, try another.

Glue

All-purpose craft glue will adhere ribbons to paper, felt, foam, and other crafting surfaces. Use it sparingly and make sure that it does not stain the ribbon. A hot glue gun and glue sticks are handy when attaching ribbons and bows to floral arrangements and home décor items. Fabric glue is the best to use to apply ribbons to fabric, trims, and leather. It grabs quickly, dries fast and clear, and is made to be washable.

Fusible web

Fusible web is a lightweight bonding agent that is activated by the heat of an iron. Placed between ribbon and fabric, the melting action causes the materials to fuse together. Fusible web is available in rolls, similar to tape, and prepackaged sheets, as well as by the yard in the interfacing department of most fabric stores. Double-stick fusible web allows for ribbons to be temporarily held in place before they are fused, and is made so it can be machine stitched without gumming the needle. Apply the web tape to the back of the ribbon, remove backing paper and place the ribbon on the project.

Press, following the manufacturer's instructions carefully for the recommended iron temperature and time needed for a good bond. Allow the fused project to cool before moving so the bond is strong. Never touch the iron directly onto the fusible web as it will melt onto the soleplate and leave a sticky residue. Protect the iron by using a pressing cloth.

Adhesive tapes

Iron-on and no-iron adhesive tapes hold like glue but without the mess, and are easy to use for attaching ribbons, especially for home décor projects. They are designed for no-sew projects and should not be stitched. Iron-on adhesive is used like fusible web tape, and is available in regular and heavy weights for different types of fabric. Peel and stick adhesive tapes are paper-backed and can be applied to one side of a ribbon. The backing paper is removed and the ribbon applied to the project.

Sealah-No-Sew tape is a double-sided, peel-and-stick, pressure-sensitive adhesive that can be lifted and repositioned until you have the ribbon placed precisely where you want it to be. After application it cures, no ironing required, within 24 hours. If desired, the project can be ironed to set the adhesive more quickly.

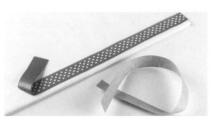

RIBBON FLOWER APPLIQUÉ TOTE BAG

Lengths of ribbons, formed, folded, and glued, create this no-sew flower tote bag.

YOU WILL NEED

- 3 yd (2.7 m) of ⅝" (15 mm) dot grosgrain ribbon for handle and flowers

- 1⅞ yd (1.7 m) of ⅝" (15 mm) grosgrain ribbon for flowers

- ⅞ yd (0.8 m) of 1½" (39 mm) grosgrain ribbon for top of bag

- 2½ yd (2.3 m) of ¼" (7 mm) green grosgrain ribbon for stems and grass

- canvas tote bag, 14" (35.6 cm) wide

- four ¾" (1.9 cm) buttons

- coordinating embroidery floss

- large-eyed needle

- fabric glue

④ Glue four double-loop petals to the top of each flower stem. Crisscross the petals to form a round flower shape.

⑤ Thread a double strand of floss through the buttons, cross in the front, and knot at the back. Glue buttons to the center of each flower

⑥ To make grass, cut two 12" (30.5 cm) and four 9" (23 cm) lengths of ¼" (7 mm) ribbon. For the flower petals, form each into double loops. Fold loops in half and glue them to the base of the flowers, adding a set on each end.

① Glue dot ribbon to bag handles. Ribbons should end about 1" (2.5 cm) from the top of the bag. Beginning at one side, glue the 1½" (39 mm) ribbon around the top of the bag, covering the raw edges of the handle ribbons. Fold back the raw edge of the ribbon and glue at the side seam.

② Following photo for placement, cut four lengths of ribbons for flower stems and glue them to the front of the bag.

③ To make each flower, cut four 8" (20.3 cm) lengths of ribbon. With each length, overlap and glue the ends, creating a circle. Fold the glued seam to the center, making a double loop petal.

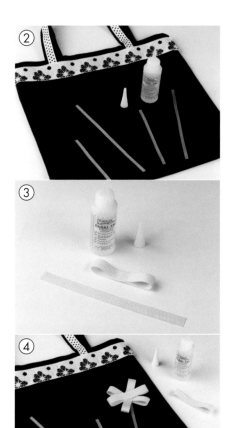

RIBBON-TABBED CURTAIN PANELS

No sewing is needed to make these easy curtain panels. Ribbons, taped to fabric lengths with Sealah adhesive, extend to form the tabs for hanging the panels from a curtain rod. Mix and match 1½" (39 mm) and ⅞" (23 mm) ribbons for a colorful effect.

YOU WILL NEED

- home décor or bottom weight cotton fabric (To determine the amount needed, measure the desired length of the finished curtains, minus 3" [7.6 cm] for the length of the ribbon tabs, plus 2" [5 cm] for the top hem, and 6" [15.2 cm] for the bottom hem. Multiply this measurement by 2 to make a pair of panels. The finished width of the panels will be the width of the fabric minus 4" [10.2 cm] for the side hems.)

- fourteen lengths of assorted ⅞" (23 mm) and 1½" (39 mm) grosgrain ribbons; to determine yardage needed of each, measure the desired length of the finished curtains, plus 14" (35.6 cm)

- Sealah adhesive tape

- iron

- 3" (7.6 cm)-wide cardboard to use as a guide for measuring tabs

- ruler

① Iron a 1" (2.5 cm) double hem along both sides of the panel fabric. Secure the hems with Sealah tape, following manufacturer's instructions.

② Iron a 1" (2.5 cm) double hem along the top edge of the panel. On the wrong side, position seven ribbon lengths. Leave an equal distance of fabric between each ribbon. Use a small piece of tape to attach the end of each ribbon to the inside of the hem.

③ Fold the top hem down and tape it to the top of the back of the panel.

④ Turn the panel right side up. Flip the ribbons to the right side. Using cardboard guide, fold each ribbon over and mark the point where the ribbon meets the top of the panel.

⑤ Apply tape to the remainder of each ribbon, and attach it down the length of the panel. Use a ruler to make sure the ribbons are straight and an equal distance from each other. Iron and tape a double 3" (7.6 cm) hem at the bottom.

②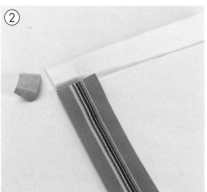

③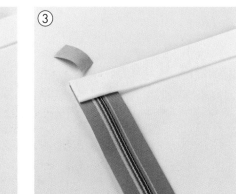

④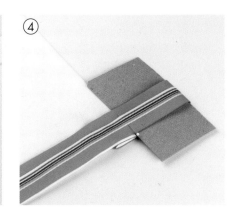

Ribbon-trimmed lamp shade

Make a coordinating lamp shade by simply taping rows of ribbons around a plain cylinder lamp shade. Start and stop the ribbons at the seam of the shade. Fold back the raw edges of the ribbons and tape for a neat finish.

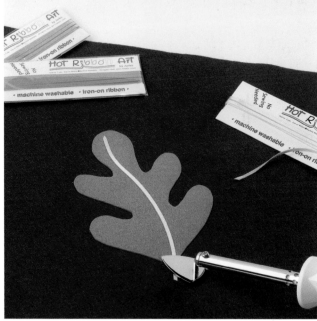

Fusible ribbon

Hot Ribbon is an adhesive-backed, machine-washable, iron-on ribbon that can add color and line to quilting, appliqué, and many other craft projects. The ⅛" (3 mm) ribbon bonds easily with a mini or regular iron, and can curve to outline shapes and add details. Follow the manufacturer's instructions for applying the ribbon to fabrics and other surfaces such as paper and wood.

RIBBON ACCESSORIES

Ribbons are to the fashion world what spices are to cuisine. They offer endless choices for color, pattern, and style, providing many ways to accessorize a wardrobe. Use ribbons to make headbands or barrettes for your hair. String ribbons with beads to make distinctive necklaces and bracelets. Need a new belt? Make one from ribbon. You can even transform your shoes with ribbon accents. Wherever you want a little extra pizzazz, create something special with ribbon.

Ribbons in Your Hair

Ribbons are the classic accessory that over the years ladies have used to style their hair. Hair bows and headbands are timeless accessories for girls of all ages. From simple and preppy to glamorous and girly, the right ribbon can complete an outfit. Of course a ribbon can just be tied on, but there are so many other hair accessories that can be made from a little bit of ribbon.

BASIC RIBBON HEADBAND

You won't need much of a 1" (2.5 cm) to 2" (5 cm) -wide ribbon to make this basic headband. Look for an interesting pattern, such as this jacquard ribbon woven with a design of chocolates. Grosgrain stripes, dots, and printed flowers also look great.

YOU WILL NEED

- ribbon for band, length determined in step 1
- 12" (30.5 cm) of elastic cord
- sewing needle and thread or sewing machine
- large eyed needle

① Measure the ribbon about 2" (5 cm) smaller than the head measurement. The ribbon will extend a few inches (centimeters) past the ears and not quite meet at the back. At each end of the ribbon, fold a double ⅜" (1 cm) hem, and stitch by hand or machine to form a small casing for the elastic.

② Cut the elastic cord in half. With large-eyed needle, thread one length through the casing at one end of the ribbon. Bring the ends together and tie them tightly into an overhand knot about 1" (2.5 cm) from the ends.

③ Trim excess cord and rotate the knot to hide it inside the casing.

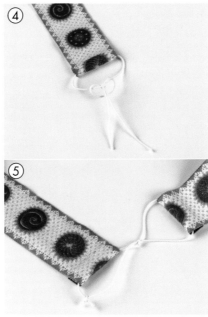

④ Fold the remaining elastic cord in half and place it under the center of the attached elastic. Bring the ends through the loop to form a lark's head knot and secure the cords to each other.

⑤ Thread one end of the second cord through the casing at the other end of the ribbon. Hold the elastic cord ends together and tie them tightly into an overhand knot about 1" (2.5 cm) from the ends. Trim excess and slide the knot into the casing.

Double-sided variation

This same technique can be made with two coordinating ribbons for a double-sided headband. Cut both ribbons the same length and seam them together at the ends. Turn right side out and press. Stitch close to both long edges and across the ends to form the casings for the elastic cord.

RIBBON-COVERED HEADBANDS

Glue method

A ribbon can be simply glued onto a blank plastic headband. Select a ribbon that is just a little wider than the headband—a ⅝" (15 mm) ribbon works well on a ½" (1.3 cm) headband. Cut a length of ribbon the measurement of the headband plus 1" (2.5 cm). Seal the ends of the ribbon to prevent fraying. Use hot glue to glue the ribbon onto the headband, turning back the raw edges and gluing them to the inside of the headband.

Sewn method

① Sew a ribbon headband cover by cutting a length of ribbon two times the measurement of the headband plus 1" (2.5 cm). Select a ribbon that is ¼" (7 mm) to ⅜" (9 mm) wider than the headband. Fold the ribbon in half, wrong sides together, and stitch close to the long edges. Straight, zigzag, or decorative edging stitches can be sewn.

② Leave the bottom of the cover open. Slide the ribbon cover onto the headband. Push the raw edges inside the cover and glue them to the headband.

③ If desired, add a basic hair bow (Bow Making, p. 50) made with matching or coordinating ribbon.

Reversible ribbon sleeve headbands

Less than ½ yard (0.5 m) each of two ribbons are sewn together to make these reversible ribbon sleeves, which easily slide on and off standard-sized plastic headbands. Of course the sleeves could be made from only one ribbon, but using two gives you twice the number of different looks. Use dots, stripes, and prints, along with solids, for a complete wardrobe of ribbon headbands.

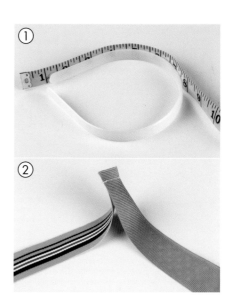

YOU WILL NEED

• plastic headband, ½" (1.3 cm) or 1" (2.5 cm)

• ½ yd (0.5 m) each of two ribbons, use ⅞" (23 mm) for a ½" (1.3 cm) headband and 1½" (39 mm) for a 1" (2.5 cm) headband

• measuring tape

• sewing machine and thread to coordinate with both ribbons

• fusible web

• iron

① Measure the outside of the headband and add 1" (2.5 cm). Cut both ribbons to this length.

② Place ribbons right side together and stitch a ¼" (7 mm) seam at one end.

③ Fold back ½" (1.3 cm) of the remaining raw edges, and fuse to hold.

④ Align long edges, wrong sides together, and pin. Starting at the seam, stitch one side close to the edge of ribbons. Stop at the end. Starting again at the seam, stitch the remaining edge and stop at the end, leaving the bottom open so that the sleeve can slide onto the headband.

Ribbon-wrapped headbands

Wrapping a headband requires a bit more ribbon than you might imagine. The exact amount will depend upon the width of the headband and the ribbon, how tightly the ribbon is wrapped, and the amount of overlap with each wrap. It is always a good idea to buy more ribbon than you think you might need. The 1" (2.5 cm) headband shown is wrapped with 2 yards (1.8 m) of ⅝" (15 mm) ribbon.

① If a soft, padded effect is desired, hot glue a strip of batting to the headband before wrapping the ribbon. Trim excess from the edges.

② Cut two 2" (5 cm) lengths of ribbon and glue them over the ends of the headband. Cut one end of the remaining ribbon on an angle, and glue it to the inside of one end of the headband. Wrap the ribbon diagonally around the headband, overlapping about ¼" (6 mm) with each wrap.

③ Continue wrapping the headband, from time to time gluing the ribbon to the inside of the headband. When you reach the end, cut the ribbon on an angle, and glue it to the inside of the headband. A bow or ribbon flowers can be glued to the wrapped headband.

RIBBON-WOVEN HEADBANDS

Lengths of ⅜" (9 mm) ribbon can be interlaced and woven onto a blank headband. By varying the number of ribbon colors used, as well as their placement, different patterns can be woven. It's fun to choose ribbon colors to match an outfit or coordinate with holiday or school colors. The sample shown is woven on a 1" (2.5 cm) headband and uses 38" (96.5 cm) each of four different ribbon colors.

① Decide which two colors you want to be the inside diamonds, and which two colors will be the outside triangles. On this headband, white and red are the inside diamonds and blue and yellow are the outside triangles.

② Overlap by ¼" (7 mm) one inside ribbon to one outside ribbon and hot glue. Glue the remaining pair or ribbons.

③ Hold the headband upside down, and position one pair of ribbons on an angle to the inside end of the headband. Add a drop of glue to hold. Position and glue the other pair on an angle to the outside end. Both inside diamond colors should be angled up.

④ Fold down the upper left ribbon over the front seam. Fold down the upper right ribbon over the back seam. A drop of glue can be added to secure the ribbons. This is the starting position. Holding the headband upside down and working from the outside of the headband, one set of ribbons will be hanging down to the right and the other set down to the left.

⑤ Fold the right front ribbon to the back of the headband. There will now be three ribbons on the left and one on the right.

⑥ Fold the remaining right ribbon to the front of the headband. All four ribbons will now be on the left. There will be an upper and lower front ribbon and an upper and lower back ribbon.

①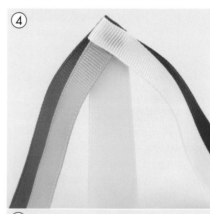

②

③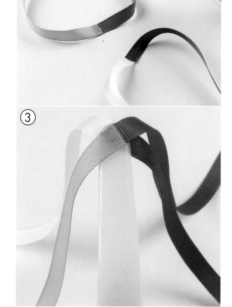

④

⑤

⑥

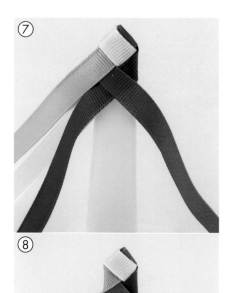

⑦

⑩

⑧

⑪

⑦ Fold the upper back ribbon to the front, placing it under the upper front ribbon and over the lower front ribbon.

⑧ Fold the upper front ribbon to the back, placing it under the lower back ribbon. You will now be back to the starting position.

⑨ Repeat steps 5 to 8 to weave the ribbons on the headband. Make sure to fold all ribbons flat against the headband. Do not let them twist. Use alligator hair clips or clothespins to hold the ribbons in place as you work. The ribbons should be woven so that the headband is completely covered and there are no gaps.

⑩ Weave the ribbons to the end of the headband and clip to hold. On the last set of steps, glue the ribbon from steps 4 and 5 to the headband. Trim excess.

⑪ Fold back and glue ribbons from steps 7 and 8 to the back of the headband, following pattern. Trim excess and seal the exposed ribbon ends to prevent raveling.

Ribbon-woven headbands color variations

This two-color variation was woven with white ribbon for the inside diamonds and black ribbon for the outside triangles.

This three-color variation was woven with pink and orange ribbons for the inside diamonds and turquoise ribbon for the outside triangles.

The contrast running stitches of the saddle-stitch grosgrain ribbons adds to the pattern of this four-color variation.

HAIR BOWS, CLIPS, AND BARRETTES

What better way to accent an outfit than wearing a coordinating ribbon hair bow, clip, or barrette? Mix and match ribbon colors and patterns for a unique and personal touch. Many of the bows shown in the Bow-Making chapter (see page 28) can be used to make hair bows. Sewn or glued onto a clip or barrette, ribbon hair bows can be made for girls from infant to adult. The selected ribbon and size of the completed bow will make the accessory appropriate for the intended wearer.

Since hair bows get a bit of wear, make sure to seal the cut edges as shown on p. 27. To prevent unsightly raveling of the ribbons, apply Fray Check or heat seal the cut ends to keep them neat. Clear nail polish can also be used. Test the sealing method on the selected ribbons before making the bow. Use hot glue or industrial glue or fabric glue to attach the bow to the clip or barrette. Allow the bow to dry and set before wearing.

Metal snap clips and fold-over plastic clips that snap together are good for small hair bows.

Pronged alligator clips open by pinching the end and are good for staying in place in fine hair. They are available in single- and double-prong styles. Alligator clips can be lined with a small strip of soft, nonslip shelf liner, carpet tape, or velvet ribbon to keep the bow from slipping.

French clip barrettes have a spring in the center that can be temporarily removed for attaching the bow.

A small strip of hook-and-loop tape can also be used to attach bows to very fine baby hair. Attach one side of the hook-and-loop tape to the bow with a few hand stitches. Place it on top of the other side with a few strands of hair between.

Look for interesting embellishments to add to the center of hair bows and ribbon-covered hair clips—buttons, beads, charms, silk flowers, etc. The scrapbook and paper-crafting section of the craft store has many unusual doodads that are fun to use with ribbon.

Ribbon-covered alligator clip

A ribbon-covered alligator clip can be worn alone or used as a base for a bow or ribbon embellishment.

YOU WILL NEED

- 4½" (11.4 cm) of ⅜" (9 mm) ribbon
- 1¾" (4.5 cm) clip
- fabric glue
- small piece of velvet ribbon (optional)

① Seal the ends of the ribbon and spread an even coat of fabric glue on the wrong side.

② Open the clip. Place the wrong side of the ribbon against the top inside of the clip.

③ Fold the ribbon to the top outside of the clip. Make sure that the edges align and the ribbons are pressed together.

④ Push the ribbon inside the hinge.

⑤ Press the rest of the ribbon to the bottom of the clip.

⑥ If desired, a small piece of velvet ribbon, shelf liner, or carpet tape can be glued to the inside top of the alligator clip.

⑦ Place a small piece of wax paper between the prongs of the clip to prevent any glue from sticking; allow glue to dry.

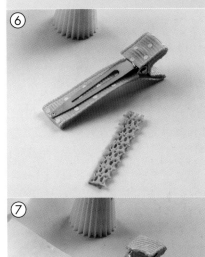

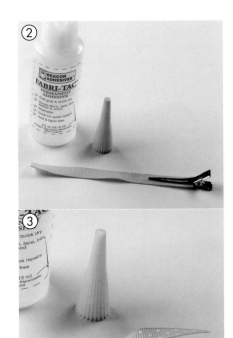

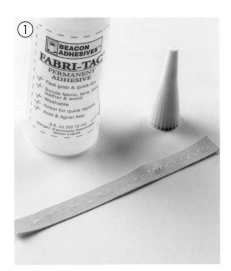

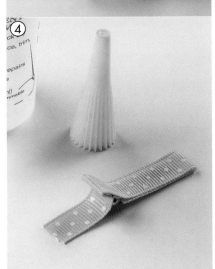

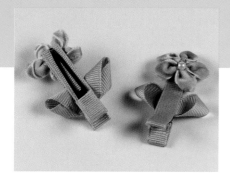

Ribbon flower alligator clips

The stem of this ribbon flower is a covered alligator clip. To make the leaves for each clip, cut two 1¾" (4.5 cm) lengths of ⅜" (9 mm) ribbon, and fold and glue them into a small leaf shape.

① Following steps 1 and 2, page 87, for covering the alligator clip, glue the stem ribbon to the inside of the clip. Glue the two leaves to the top of the clip, at the base of the hinge.

② Continue to glue the stem ribbon to the top of the clip and around the hinge. Glue a small premade ribbon flower to the end of the clip.

BASIC HAIR BOWS: BUTTERFLY BOW VARIATION ✂

The basic hair bow (page 50), with or without surrounding loops, is a versatile bow for various types of ribbons in different widths. By experimenting with coordinating patterns and embellishments, many styles of ribbon hair bows can be created.

With a little adjustment, the basic hair bow technique is used to make these butterfly bows. Each butterfly uses 16" (40.6 cm) of ⅝" (15 mm) ribbon or 18" (45.7 cm) of ⅞" (23 mm) ribbon for the wings, 4" (10.2 cm) of ⅛" (3 mm) black grosgrain for the antennae, 4½" (11.4 cm) of ⅜" (9 mm) black grosgrain for the body and one 1¾" (4.5 cm) alligator clip.

① Follow the directions for making the basic hair bow. Instead of marking the center of the ribbon, mark the ⅝" (15 mm) ribbon 9" (23 cm) from one end. (Mark the ⅞" [23 mm] ribbon 10" [25.4 cm] from one end.) When the loops are formed, the top loop will be a little larger than the bottom loop.

② Tie the bow to create the butterfly wings.

③ Cut two 2" (5 cm) lengths of ⅛" (3 mm) black ribbon. Fold each in half. Open the clip and glue them to the inside of the top section of the clip. Make sure to angle them off to each side a little so they will not interfere with the body ribbon that will be glued to the top of the clip.

④ Open clip and glue the ⅜" (9 mm) ribbon to the inside of the top. Glue the bow to the middle of the outside of the clip. Bring the ⅜" (9 mm) ribbon over the edge of the clip and glue it to the top of the clip over the center of the bow.

⑤ Continue to glue the ribbon around the hinge and to the back of the clip.

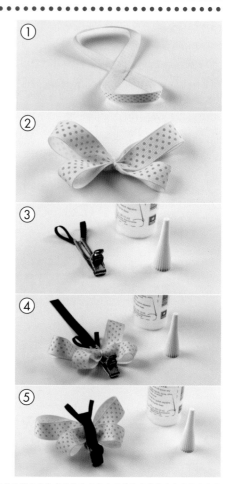

Ribbon-covered snap clip

A covered metal snap clip, wrapped with ¼" (7 mm) ribbon, makes an attractive hair clip base for a small bow or other embellishment.

YOU WILL NEED

- 15" (38.1 cm) of ribbon
- metal snap clip
- hot glue gun

①

②

③

④

⑤

⑥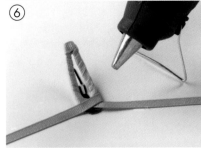

⑦

⑧

⑨

① Open snap. Hot glue the center of the ribbon length to the narrow tip of the clip. Fold the right ribbon behind the clip at an angle.

② Bring that same ribbon around and through the middle of the clip. Pull the ribbon so it lies at an angle tight against the clip.

③ Following the same angle, wrap the ribbon down the left side of the clip. Pull tightly with each wrap and make sure the ribbon overlaps slightly so the clip does not show.

④ At the end of the clip, bring the ribbon diagonally across the wide end of the clip and glue.

⑤ Go back to the narrow tip of the clip. In the same way, wrap the right side of the clip.

⑥ Glue the right side ribbon across the wide end of the clip, forming an X with the left-side ribbon.

⑦ With the clip facing with the wide end down, bring the ribbon on the left to the back of the clip and back through the center.

⑧ Bring that ribbon to the back of the clip and glue. Trim excess ribbon and seal the end.

⑨ In the same manner, wrap and finish the right-side ribbon.

⑩ Glue a small bow or other embellishment to the wide end of the clip.

Loopy barrette

This loopy barrette is made by stitching loops of ribbon onto a French clip barrette. The barrette shown is made with ¾ yard (0.7 m) each of six ⅜" (9 mm) ribbons. You can make the bow with any width and number of ribbons. The amount needed will depend upon how many and how big you want the loops to be.

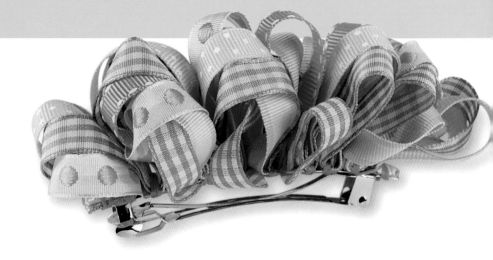

YOU WILL NEED

- French clip barrette
- ribbons of your choice
- needle and thread
- Fray Check

① Remove barrette spring and set aside. Prepare the needle by threading two long strands of thread through the eye and doubling them so that there are a total of four threads. Stack the ribbons one on top of the other and insert the needle through the stack about ¼" (7 mm) from one end. Sew the stack of ribbons to the barrette, through the hole at the hinge end.

② Turn the barrette so the flat size is up. Dropping the needle and holding the thread with your hand, tightly wrap the thread several times around the base of the hinge.

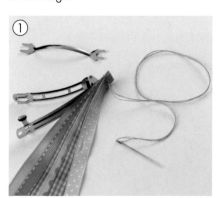

③ Holding the stack of ribbons and keeping tension on the thread, form a loop about 1½" (3.8 cm) tall. Place the bottom of the loop against the top of the barrette. Wrap the thread around the ribbons and barrette to hold.

④ Holding the thread tight, continue to make loops, wrapping each to the barrette. Each loop should be alternately angled slightly up and down.

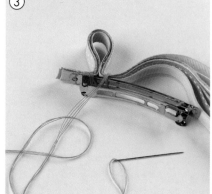

⑤ At the end, stitch the ribbons to the barrette and trim excess. Turn the bow so the underside is up. Use the remaining thread to sew back and forth to the other end to make sure that the loops are secure and will not move. Knot at the end and secure. Seal the ribbon ends with Fray Check. Replace the barrette spring and pull out ribbon loops for a full bow. If desired, a length of ribbon can be glued to the inside of the barrette to cover the thread.

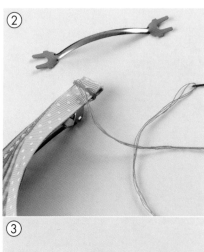

KORKER RIBBON AND KORKER BOWS

Curly korker ribbon is made by wrapping ribbon onto a dowel and heat setting in the oven. You must use 100% polyester ribbon, ¼" (7 mm) or ⅜" (9 mm) grosgrain works great.

YOU WILL NEED

- about 1 yard (0.9 m) of polyester ribbon, ¼" (7 mm) or ⅜" (9 mm) wide
- 18" (45.7 cm) dowel, ¼" (6 mm) diameter
- two wooden clothespins
- aluminum foil
- oven

① Start at one end by securing the ribbon to the dowel with a clothespin. Make sure to use an unpainted wood clothespin that can take the heat of the oven. Twist the dowel with one hand as you wrap the ribbon tightly along the length of the dowel. Place the wraps side by side without overlapping. The tighter you roll the ribbon onto the dowel, the tighter the curl will be.

② Secure the other end of the ribbon with another clothespin.

③ Line the center oven rack with aluminum foil and preheat the oven to 275°F (135°C). Place the wrapped dowels into the oven and bake 15 to 20 minutes. Carefully remove the dowels from the oven and allow them to cool before handling. Remove the clothespins and gently unravel the korker ribbon off the dowel.

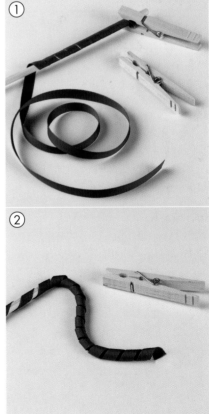

①

②

Short lengths of korker ribbons were added to the center of this bow before it was sewn to a stretchy knit headband.

Ribbon Jewelry

Ribbons add color and texture to jewelry designs. They can be threaded through beads, rings, and chain, wrapped and braided, or strung with pearls and crystals to create a variety of unique accessories.

THREADING BEADS AND OTHER THINGS ONTO RIBBON

Threading beads onto ribbon requires a bit of experimentation to determine the best width and type of ribbon for the selected beads and the intended look of the completed design. Crystal beads threaded onto organza ribbon create a feminine, dressy effect. Big, chunky felt or crochet beads threaded onto taffeta or soft narrow grosgrain will make a more casual piece.

The holes of most beads are usually too small to use a needle for threading the ribbon. Floss threaders, sold where you would find toothbrushes and dental floss, are the perfect solution. They are fine and easily compress to pass a ribbon through the bead's hole. Of course some ribbons are too wide and thick to use for threading. Test the selected beads on a few types of ribbons and widths to find the best combination.

Using the floss threader as a needle, insert the end of the threader through the bead and pull the ribbon through. If the ribbon fits snugly in the bead hole, the beads can be spaced out along the ribbon and will stay in position.

Crochet-covered beads were threaded with a floss threader onto narrow

checked ribbon to make this necklace. Small lengths of ribbon were knotted at each end of the beads to add additional interest. The necklace is long enough that a clasp is not necessary so the ribbon ends were simply knotted together with an overhand knot.

For a classic look, thread grosgrain ribbon onto a length of chain. Look for a flat chain that has openings large enough for the ribbon to pass in and out between the links. This choker was made from an old chain necklace. The clasp was removed and ⅜" (9 mm) grosgrain was threaded through the links. To prevent the chain from slipping down the ribbon, the end links were stitched to the ribbon. The ribbon ends serve as the clasp and can be worn tied at the back, front, or off to one side.

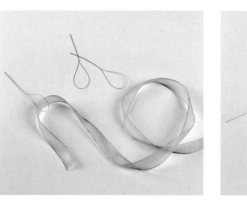

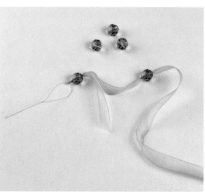

RIBBON CLAMPS ✄

A ribbon necklace can be worn with the ribbon ends simply tied in a knot or a bow. This allows for the necklace to be adjustable in length. A tied bow can add interest to the design. Remember to seal any exposed raw ribbon edges.

For a more finished appearance, a ribbon clamp and jewelry clasp can be attached to the ends. Ribbon clamps, also known as ribbon crimps or ribbon ends, are available in several styles, metals, and various sizes for different widths of ribbon. The ribbon clamps have small teeth inside that will hold tight when the clamps are closed onto the ends of the ribbon.

① Fold back and glue the raw edge of the ribbon the small amount that will fit inside the clamp. Use jewelry pliers to squeeze the edges of the clamp together, completely hiding the raw edge, and holding the clamp securely.

② Use a jump ring to attach the loop on the clamp to one side of a jewelry clasp.

① ②

Just a few beautiful ribbons and a special pendant are all that is needed to make a one-of-a-kind necklace. The hand-dyed silk and sheer ribbons used for this necklace were centered and threaded onto a floss threader and brought through the hole in the pendant. The floss threader was cut off and the ribbons were attached to the pendant with a lark's head knot. Ribbon clamps finish the ends.

STRINGING RINGS ONTO A RIBBON

A quick and easy necklace or bracelet can be made by stringing a few flat rings, washers, or even soda can pop tops onto a length of ribbon. Select a width of ribbon that fits the center of the ring.

① Thread the first ring onto the ribbon from back to front. Add the second ring by threading the ribbon through front to back. Slide the second ring over the edge of the first ring. Bring the ribbon through the center of the first ring, front to back.

② Bring the ribbon through the center of the second ring from back to front. Add the third ring by bringing the ribbon through from front to back, and overlapping the right side of the third ring over the left side of the second.

③ Bring the ribbon back though the second ring from front to back. Bring the thread through the center of the third ring from back to front. Continue these steps to add additional rings, always overlapping the next ring over the previous one.

STRINGING BEADS WITH RIBBON

Incorporating ribbons into strung beaded jewelry designs adds color and interest to the piece. By adding ribbons, fewer beads may be needed as they can be featured on only part of the bracelet or necklace. One of the most enjoyable aspects of planning these projects is choosing the type and color of ribbons that will go with the selected beads. Because both sides of the ribbon may show, select a double-sided ribbon such as grosgrain, taffeta, or double-faced satin.

Standard beading thread is best to use for threading the ribbons and beads because it is stronger than regular sewing thread. Select a color thread that matches the ribbon being used. Use a fine sewing needle instead of a beading needle, and make sure that it is small enough to pass through the holes in the beads. A sewing needle will go through the ribbon better and is stronger than a beading needle. Use the thread doubled and knotted in the needle. The thread can be waxed but take care that not too much wax is applied so it does not collect on the ribbon as the needle passes through.

ZIGZAG RIBBON BEADING

With this technique, a zigzag pattern will be formed as the ribbon alternates from side to side between beads.

(1) Decide where you want to begin adding beads onto the ribbon and insert the needle at that point. Take a small stitch back into the ribbon and string on the first bead. The bead will come down to cover the knot.

(2) Bring the working end of the ribbon up over the ribbon and insert the needle where the hole meets the ribbon. Let the ribbon hang over the top of the bead. Take a few small stitches to hold the ribbon in place against the bead.

(3) Thread the next bead onto the needle and bring it down to meet the ribbon. Bring the ribbon up and over the bead and insert the needle where the hole meets the ribbon. Take a few small stitches to hold.

(4) Continue adding beads in this way for the desired length. Keep checking to make sure that enough ribbon has been placed around each bead so that the beads are lying in a straight line.

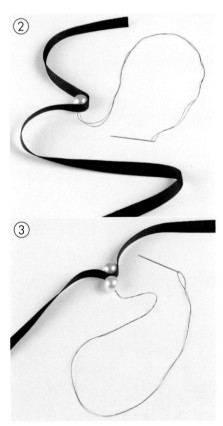

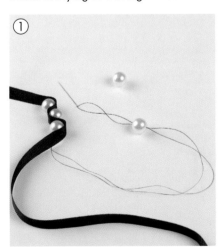

This necklace was made from 1 yard (0.9 m) of ⅝" (15 mm) sheer ribbon and graduated sizes of pearls. The bracelet was strung with a fine stretchy elastic cord. The ends were knotted securely, trimmed, and the excess ribbon was tied in a bow to cover the knot.

SCALLOP RIBBON BEADING

If the ribbon is kept to one side as the beads are added, a scallop pattern will form.

① Decide where you want to begin adding beads onto the ribbon, and insert the needle at that point. Fold the ribbon back on itself and take a few small stitches at the fold to hide the knot.

② Thread the first bead onto the thread and bring the working end of the ribbon up to the top hole of the bead. Insert the needle into the ribbon and take a small stitch. Fold the ribbon back onto itself at this point. Take another small stitch to secure the thread and tighten the ribbon against the bead.

③ Add the second bead in the same way, keeping the ribbon folded back in the same direction so that the ribbon remains on only one side of the beads.

④ Continue adding beads in this way for the desired length. From time to time, check to make sure that enough ribbon has been placed against each bead and the beads are lying straight.

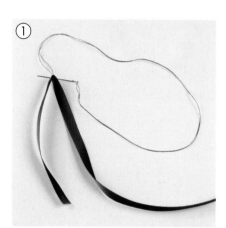

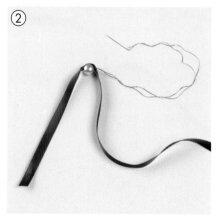

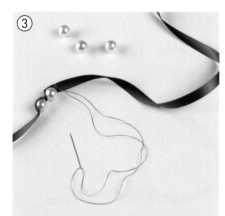

FREE-FORM RIBBON BEADING

If the ribbon is not placed directly against the beads and is twisted, folded, turned, and pleated as it is stitched, a free-form ribbon beading pattern will be created.

The ribbon does not have to be threaded throughout the design. Different colors and types of narrow ribbons are folded back and forth into loopy bows and threaded onto the needle as the beads are added for this necklace.

RIBBON-WRAPPED BANGLE BRACELETS

Plain wood bangles are the perfect base for a ribbon-wrapped bracelet. The craft stores carry ready-to-decorate unfinished wood bangles in several styles and sizes.

Use ⅜" (9 mm) to ⅝" (15 mm) ribbon for wrapping. The amount needed will depend upon the size of the bracelet, the width of the ribbon, and how closely the ribbon is wrapped. Keep the rows of wrapping even and make sure that the bracelet is completely covered without any gaps. The bangles can be wrapped with one or more colors of ribbons. Rows of ribbon wrapping can be spaced out or overlapped, and narrow ribbons can be wrapped over wider ribbons. Buttons or beads can be threaded onto ⅛" ribbon and added on top of a wrapped ribbon bangle. A braid of ribbon can be made and glued around the wrapped bangle. Mix and match ribbons to create an armful of coordinating bracelets.

YOU WILL NEED

- plain wood bangle
- ribbon as described above
- tacky glue
- spray sealer (optional)

① To begin, cut the end of the ribbon on a slight angle and glue it to the inside of the bangle with tacky glue. Wrap the ribbon around the bracelet, making sure the wraps are even and the ribbon lies flat against the bracelet. From time to time, add a drop of glue to the back of the bracelet to keep the ribbon in place.

② At the end of the wrapping, neatly overlap and glue the ribbon over the beginning end. If desired, spray the wrapped bangle with a sealer to add a finish and keep the ribbons clean. Test the sealer first to make sure it does not change the appearance of the ribbons.

RIBBON CUFF BRACELET

This bracelet is a great way to show off a short piece of special ribbon. Buttons and beads can be added or the beauty of the special ribbon alone can be the main feature.

① Cut the grosgrain ribbon in half. Place the feature ribbon over one length of the wider ribbon, and hand- or machine-stitch close to the sides.

② Right sides together, place the remaining grosgrain ribbon length on top of the stitched ribbon. Stitch a narrow seam along one end.

③ Fold the ribbons right side out. Align the sides and stitch close to the edges.

④ Stitch the remaining raw edges together with zigzag or overcast stitches to prevent raveling.

⑤ Stitch hook-and-loop tape at each end so that the seamed end of the cuff overlaps the overcast end.

⑥ Sew buttons and beads onto the cuff, if desired.

③

④
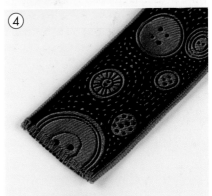

①

②

⑤

YOU WILL NEED

- 9" (22.9 cm) of a special ribbon

- 18" (45.7 cm) of a slightly wider grosgrain ribbon

- sewing machine or needle and thread

- hook and loop tape

- buttons or beads (optional)

YOU WILL NEED

- 2 yd (1.8 m) each of four grosgrain ribbons, ¼" (7 mm) wide
- needle and thread
- fabric glue

RIBBON LANYARD BRACELET

The same braid you may have made at scout camp with plastic laces can be woven with ribbons. Four different colors of ¼" (7 mm) grosgrain ribbon are used to make this bracelet. The ribbons are braided together on each side of the center point of the ribbons with a square or box stitch. The braid is twisted before the ends are sewn together to create the spiral design. This lanyard braid has a great deal of stretch and will fit over your hand and then return to its original shape when worn on the wrist.

① ② ③

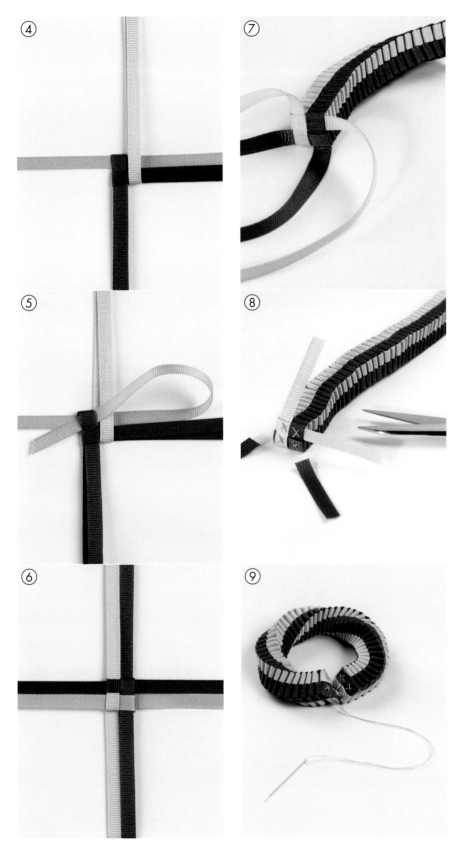

④

⑤

⑥

⑦

⑧

⑨

① Cut four lengths of ribbon each 2 yd (1.8 m) long. Overlap the centers as shown to create a woven square. Secure the ribbons by hand-tacking them with a needle and thread, or adding a drop of glue where each ribbon overlaps.

② In this sample, the purple ribbon will be ribbon A, dark green will be ribbon B, lavender will be ribbon C, and lime will be ribbon D. Working in a counter-clockwise direction, fold the ribbons over one another. Begin with A over D (purple over lime).

③ Then fold B over A (dark green over purple).

④ Fold C over B (lavender over dark green).

⑤ Fold D over C (lime over lavender) and under the loop formed by A. Tighten up the ribbons after each round of weaving.

⑥ Reverse the pattern and work in a clockwise direction to fold D over A, C over D, B over D, then A over B and through the loop formed by D. This returns the ribbons to their original positions.

⑦ Repeat from the beginning, working alternately in counterclockwise and clockwise rounds until the braid measures 3½" (8.9 cm).

⑧ Returning to the starting point where the ribbons were first overlapped, weave the other four ribbon ends in the same pattern for 3½" (8.9 cm). The finished length of the braid should be 7" (17.8 cm). To secure the ribbons at both ends, sew a small cross stitch through each of the four end squares, and cut the ribbon close to the weaving.

⑨ Give the braid a full twist and butt the two ends together and slipstitch to hold.

REVERSIBLE RIBBON WATCHBAND OR BRACELET

Make a reversible watchband or bracelet from two sturdy coordinating ribbons—grosgrains are a good choice. Both ribbons need to be the same width. Choose a pair of D-rings that corresponds to the width of the ribbons.

YOU WILL NEED

- two ribbons of the same width
- two D-rings in same width as ribbons
- sewing machine or needle and thread
- watch (optional)

① Measure your wrist and add 2½" (6.4 cm). Cut each ribbon to that measurement. Right sides together, stitch the ribbons at one end in a ¼" (6 mm) seam. Slip both D-rings onto the ribbons.

② Right sides together, stitch the ribbons at the other end in a ¼" (6 mm) seam.

③ Turn ribbons right side out. Slide the D-rings into position at one seam, making sure the flat side of the rings is against the seam. Align the long edges of the ribbons and pin.

④ Starting at the end without the rings, neatly stitch down one long side, close to the edge of the ribbons. Continue stitching across the ribbons about ⅝" (15 mm) from the seam with the rings and then back up the remaining edge. If using as a watchband, slip watch onto ribbon.

①

②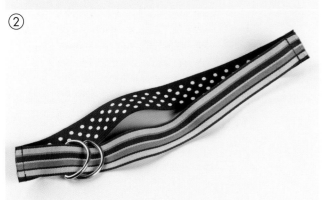

③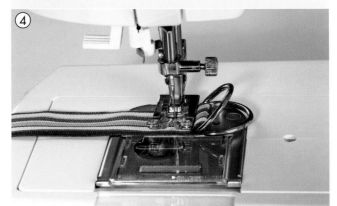

④

Belts, Shoes, and More
RIBBON D-RING BELT

Ribbon belts made with D-ring buckles are so easy to make that you can have one to match every outfit. Almost any sturdy ribbon can be used—from classic striped grosgrains to fun prints and fancy brocades. Choose a pair of D-rings that corresponds to the width of the selected ribbon.

YOU WILL NEED

- ribbon
- two D-rings in same width as ribbon
- sewing machine

① Measure the waist of the wearer or the waistband of a garment for which you are making the belt. Add 10" (25.4 cm). Cut the ribbon two times that measurement and fold it in half. Pin the sides together.

② Starting at the folded edge, neatly machine-stitch down one side of the folded ribbon. Continue to stitch near the raw edges and up the remaining long edge. Keep the stitches straight and close to the edges of the ribbons.

③ Thread the cut ribbon end through both D-rings. Fold the raw edges under ¼" (6 mm) and then fold them down about ¾" (1.9 cm). Stitch the folded edge to hold the rings securely in place.

Ribbon and webbing belt

Ribbon and webbing belts are easy to make with a military-style slide buckle. Stitch a ⅞" (23 mm) grosgrain ribbon onto 1" (2.5 cm) belt webbing, zigzag stitching at the ends to prevent any raveling. Use jewelry pliers to attach the webbing clamp to one end. Insert the other end into the slide buckle, and fold the clamp portion back to hold it secure.

RIBBON-TRIMMED SOCKS

Save on the cost of boutique socks by sewing a length of ribbon onto inexpensive plain cuffed socks.

① To determine how much ribbon is needed, fully stretch the top of the sock and measure. Add ½" (1.3 cm) for a seam allowance. Cut two lengths of ribbon that measurement for each pair of socks.

② Seal the raw edges of the ribbon. Sew the ends together to form a ring.

③ Turn the sock inside out. Place the right side of the ribbon loop against the edge of the sock. Pin the seam at the back of the sock. Stretch the top of the sock and pin the edge of the ribbon at the front of the sock. Stretch the sock and pin the ribbon at the approximate sides of the sock. This does not have to be an exact measurement. The pins are there to help the ribbon stay in place as it is being sewn.

④ With a zigzag stitch, sew the ribbon to the top of the sock, overcasting the edge. Stretch the top of the sock as you sew to each pin.

⑤ Turn the sock right side out and fold down the ribbon-trimmed cuff.

②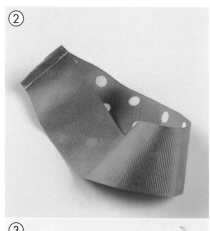

④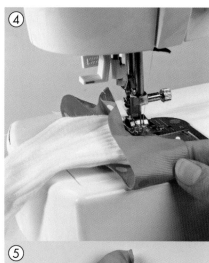

①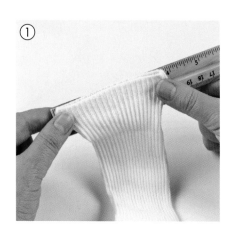

③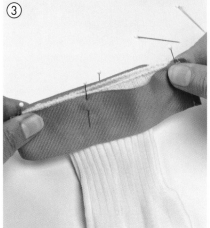

⑤

RIBBONS ON YOUR SHOES

Use a little ribbon to customize shoes to match any outfit or suit your mood.

Whether dressy or casual, a ribbon bow at the heel or toe of a shoe makes a fashion statement.

To create different looks for one pair of shoes, sew bows and ribbon rosettes to shoe clips. These small fold-over metal clips have holes for sewing and simply fold over and clip to the front of the shoe.

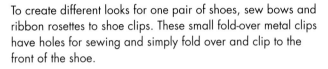

Sneakers can be princess or preppy with ribbons used for laces. Seal the ends to prevent raveling or tie them into a knot near the ends.

Plain flip-flops are the perfect beginning for fun, fabulous footwear. Wrap the straps with ribbon or cover them with a ribbon-loop braid (Ribbon Trims, page 120.) Use glue specifically made for gluing flip-flops. It is strong and flexible and will hold up to wear. Short lengths of ribbon can also be simply tied onto the straps—a great way to use up little bits of ribbon.

RIBBONS FOR YOUR FAVORITE POOCH

Create a fun and colorful ribbon collar and leash for your favorite dog. Reflective ribbon, as well as grosgrains and jacquards, are good choices.

YOU WILL NEED

- 1" (2.5 cm) webbing
- ⅝" (15 mm) to ⅞" (23 mm) ribbon
- parachute buckle
- one D-ring

②

③

④

① Measure the dog's neck and add 6" (15.2 cm). Cut the webbing and ribbon to that measurement. Fuse or stitch the ribbon onto the webbing and heat-seal or overcast the ends to prevent raveling.

② Following manufacturer's instructions, slip one end of the ribbon-covered webbing into the male side of parachute clip. Fold back the webbing 3" (7.6 cm) and stitch across the webbing close to the clip and close to the cut end.

③ Test the collar size on the dog and note how much webbing should be folded back on the other side to have a good fit. Slip the D-ring onto the webbing and attach it to the female side of the clip.

④ Stitch across the webbing close to the clip. Slide the D-ring up, and stitch across the webbing about ¾" (1.9 cm) from the first stitching, to hold the D-ring in place. Stitch across the webbing close to the cut end.

To make a coordinating leash, stitch ribbon to webbing of the desired length; seal the cut ends to prevent raveling. Attach one end to a swivel hook and sew securely. Fold a loop with the other end, and stitch securely.

Make little bows for furry dogs by forming the ribbon into a bow, stitching the loops at the center, and then stitching the bow around a tiny rubber band—either dental rubber bands or the small ones used for holding thin braids.

CRAFTING WITH RIBBON

Ribbons are one of the most versatile crafting materials. With the wide variety of widths and patterns available, ribbons can set a mood, complement a design, and also be functional. Sometimes just one favorite ribbon can be the inspiration for an entire project. Many of the ribbon techniques presented in previous chapters can be applied to different surfaces. Embellishing scrapbook pages, handmade cards, and paper crafts with ribbons is very popular. Ribbons can also be attached to wood, plastic, and ceramic, and incorporated into home décor accessories. Ribbons add depth and texture and the extra accent to make a project special.

Ribbon weaving and patchwork techniques (pages 146 and 158) can be applied to paper to create one-of-a-kind greeting cards. A ribbon flower (see ribbon flower appliqué tote bag on page 175) coordinates with the paper decoupaged to this clipboard.

Check the paper crafting and scrapbook supply sections of the craft store when looking for ribbons. There you will find ribbons with interesting themes and patterns, often designed to coordinate with printed papers and other embellishments.

Attaching Ribbons to Paper
GLUE IT DOWN

When you just want to stick it in place, double sided tape or adhesive glue dots are the simple and easy method. Glue is too messy. Put the tape on the ribbon or run the glue dot dispenser on the back of the ribbon and place it on the project. Alternatively, the tape or dots can be positioned onto the working surface and the ribbon put on top. Ribbons can also be run through a sticker-making and laminating machine and made into a sticker.

The raw edges of the ribbon can be turned to the back of the paper. Or, the ends can be cut on an angle or into a V. Knots can be tied along the length for an added embellishment detail. Ribbon can also be folded and taped into zigzag patterns or mitered around corners.

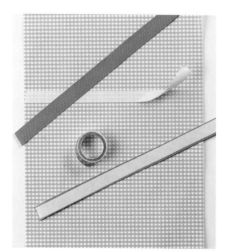

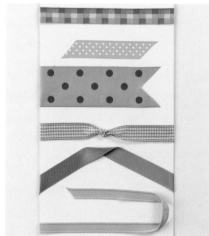

THREADED THROUGH PUNCHED OPENINGS

A standard round paper punch can be used to make a hole for threading or tying ribbons onto paper.

This easy bow embellishment is made without having to tie any knots.

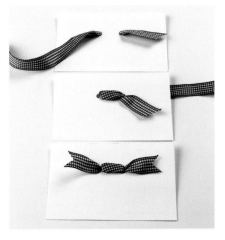

Punch two holes into the paper the desired distance apart. Thread the ribbon though one hole and out through the other. Bring the ribbon back through the first hole. Thread it through the second hole again to complete the bow. Trim excess ribbon.

Decorative brads can be added at the point where a ribbon is threaded into a punched hole.

Ribbon-stitch punches cut parallel slots that can be used for weaving ribbons onto paper. There are many different types and sizes to accommodate various widths of ribbon. Intricate decorative punches are also interesting to use for paper and ribbon projects. Ribbon can be placed behind the cut edges to showcase the designs. Punches can be combined to create paper lace.

Thread and weave ribbons through punched holes to make simple or intricate designs for cards and other paper crafts.

SLIPPED THROUGH CUT SLITS

A simple way to add a ribbon is to slip it through slits that have been cut into the paper background. Use a sharp craft knife, cutting board, and a ruler to make the slits the exact length of the ribbon width.

Just a short length of jacquard ribbon was used to decorate this happy birthday card. Slits were cut into the pink dot paper at the points where the ribbon will enter and exit the paper. The cut ribbon ends are taped to the back of the paper.

This initial picture was made by slipping ribbon through slits cut into background paper. Use lengths of ribbon, or paper cut the exact width of the ribbon, to plan the design. Measure to make sure the monogram is symmetrical.

① Make a pattern indicating where the slits need to be cut.

② Place the pattern over the background paper and use a pin to mark the end of each slit that needs to be cut. Using a craft knife held against a ruler, connect the dots and cut the slits.

③ Insert the ribbon into the slits and tape the cut ends to the back of the paper.

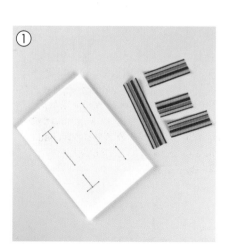

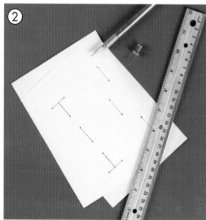

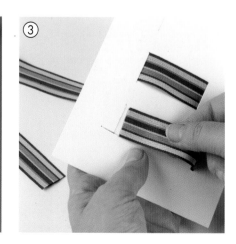

Ribbon Embellishments
RIBBON CORNERS

Like vintage photo corners, decorative ribbon corners elegantly embellish and hold a card or picture. By folding ribbon lengths around the right-angle edge of a picture or card, the corners can be taped directly to the picture. Or, they can be made functional by taping them only to the background paper so that the item can be removed and reinserted. This is a nice way to display a note or card on a scrapbook page so it can be opened and read.

Center a length of ribbon across the corner of the paper. Fold the ends back smooth against each edge and tape to hold.

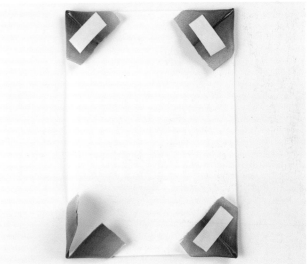

RIBBON TABS AND TAILS

Small ribbon tabs can organize a journal or encourage interaction on a scrapbook page.

To form the tabs, a small length of ribbon is folded in half and taped between two layers of paper. Ribbon tails are made by threading a folded length of ribbon through a punched hole and then passing the ends through the loop.

RIBBON SLIDES AND CHARMS

Decorative ribbon slides look like small belt buckles, and are available in different styles, sizes, and materials. Slide them onto a length of ribbon to add an accent detail.

Instead of a bow, decorate a gift box with a ribbon slide and charms. The charms can be attached to the ribbon with jewelry glue that is made for gluing metal. Charms can also be attached to the slide with jump rings.

Coordinating paper, ribbons, and slides were used to decorate this clipboard. A clipboard with a removable clip makes it easy to apply the background paper with decoupage glue. Another layer of paper, decorated with rows of ribbon, was added as a bottom pocket. Ribbon was wrapped and glued around a pencil, and attached to the board through a ribbon slide glued to the clip.

Frame charms are positioned on these cards to showcase the special ribbons.

Printing on Ribbon

Several methods can be used to add printed designs to ribbon. All of these techniques are designed to be used on ribbon projects that will not be washed.

RUBBER STAMPS

Adding ribbons to a rubber stamped image can add texture and detail. Sheer and brocade ribbons, as well as ribbon roses, were glued to the stamped and embossed wreath design on this card.

Stamp directly onto plain ribbon to create patterned ribbon. Use inks that are designed to work on fabric. Temporarily tape the ribbon onto scrap paper with removable double-sided tape. Stamp the ribbon, allowing the images to extend beyond the edges, if desired. When dry, heat set with a dry, hot iron using a press cloth.

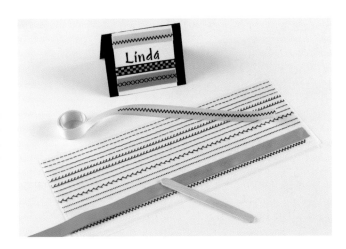

CLEAR STICKERS

For cardmaking or scrapbooking, clear stickers can be placed onto ribbon. Make sure that the color of the selected ribbon contrasts with the print of the sticker so the details of the image are clear.

RUB-ONS

Rub-on designs can be placed onto ribbon and transferred by rubbing the back of the design with a flat stick.

PRINTING RIBBON WITH A COMPUTER AND PRINTER

Computer text can be printed directly onto short lengths of ribbon.

① Choose a light-colored ribbon that is thin and will lie flat against paper when it is run through the printer. Compose your message and format it in the style and size that will fit the width of the selected ribbon. Print the message onto plain paper.

② Apply removable double-sided tape to the back of the ribbon and position it over the words just printed. You can usually see through the ribbon to help center the message. Press the ribbon firmly to the paper to remove any ripples. The ribbon must lie perfectly flat against the paper so that it will not get caught while passing through the printer.

③ Place the paper back into the printer, and print the document again. Test the printing with different settings to get the best results. Some ribbons may bleed or streak with different settings. Wiping the ribbon before printing with Perfect Printing Pouch powder will help to bond the ink to the ribbon and produce a clearer print.

④ Separate the ribbon from the paper and remove the tape if it sticks to the back of the printed ribbon.

① ②

③ ④

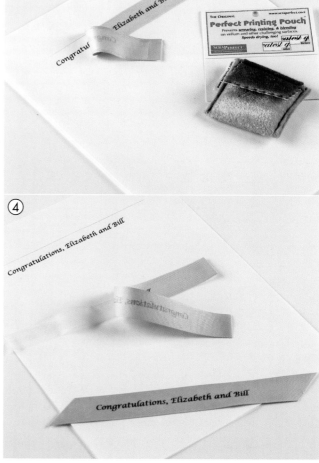

DESIGN RUNNER ✂

The Design Runner is a small portable printer that can print designs and messages onto ribbon, as well as paper and other surfaces. Follow the manufacturer's instructions carefully and test the printing on the selected ribbon. Use the Perfect Printing Pouch if necessary for a sharper print.

Customized printed ribbon is great for gift wrapping, party decorations, and favors.

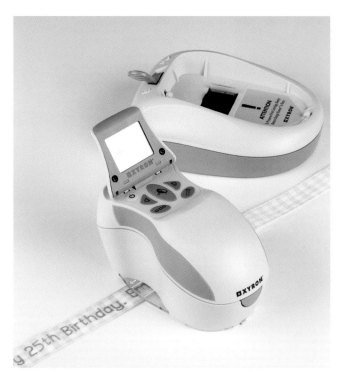

Wedding wand

Wave and greet the happy couple as they leave the wedding ceremony with this celebration ribbon wand. Cut a 12" (30.5 cm) length of ⅜" (1 cm) dowel and paint it to match the ribbon colors. Add a screw eye to one end. If desired, wrap the dowel with ribbon and glue the ends to hold. Cut 1-yard (0.9 m) lengths of different ribbons, including one that has been printed with a special message to commemorate the day. Thread the ribbons through the screw eye and tie them in a knot at the center to hold.

Attaching Ribbons to Other Materials

Ribbons can be secured to wood, plastic, ceramic, and other smooth surfaces with Sealah adhesive tape.

Follow manufacturer's instructions to apply ribbon lengths to painted wood letters.

Tape lengths of ribbon to a square ceramic vase and create a custom floral arrangement to match dining table placemats.

RIBBON MEMO BOARD

A French ribbon memo board is a classic ribbon craft. Card, photos, notes, and other mementoes can be tucked and clipped onto the crossed ribbons. Begin with a purchased covered bulletin board or cover a cork board or piece of foam board with a layer of batting and fabric. Criss-cross lengths of ribbons across the board and glue the cut ends to the back. At the points where the ribbons cross, sew a button or glue them to the fabric to hold the ribbons in place. If desired, rows of wide ribbon can be glued along the bottom and side edges to create narrow pockets at the bottom.